Qt for Symbian

Qt for Symbian

Edited by:

Frank H.P. Fitzek

Tony Torp

Tommi Mikkonen

A John Wiley and Sons, Ltd, Publication

This edition first published 2010
© 2010 John Wiley & Sons, Ltd.

Registered office John Wiley & Sons Ltd, The Atrium, Southern Gate, Chichester, West Sussex, PO19 8SQ, United Kingdom.

For details of our global editorial offices, for customer services and for information about how to apply for permission to reuse the copyright material in this book please see our website at www.wiley.com.

ISBN 978-0-470-75010-0

A catalogue record for this book is available from the British Library.

Set in 10/12pt Times by Sunrise Setting Ltd, Torquay, UK.
Printed in the Great Britain by TJ International Ltd, Padstow, Cornwall.

CONTENTS

6   Qt Apps and Native Symbian Extensions   **95**
Angelo Perkusich, Kyller Costa Gorgônio and Hyggo Oliveira de Almeida

7   Qt for Symbian Examples   **117**
Bertalan Forstner, András Berke, Imre Kelényi, Morten V. Pedersen and Hassan Charaf

CONTRIBUTORS

Frank H.P. Fitzek
Aalborg University
Niels Jernes Vej 12
DK-9220 Aalborg
Denmark
ff@es.aau.dk

Tony Torp
TAMK University of Applied Sciences
Teiskontie 33
FI-33520 Tampere
Finland
tony.torp@tamk.fi

Tommi Mikkonen
Tampere University of Technology
Korkeakoulunkatu 1
FI-33720 Tampere
Finland
tjm@cs.tut.fi

Morten V. Pedersen
Aalborg University
Mobile Device Group
Niels Jernes Vej 12
DK-9220 Aalborg
Denmark
mvp@es.aau.dk

Janus Heide
Aalborg University
Mobile Device Group
Niels Jernes Vej 12
DK-9220 Aalborg
Denmark
jah@es.aau.dk

Andreas Jakl
Upper Austria University of Applied Sciences,
Campus Hagenberg
Softwarepark 11
4232 Hagenberg
Austria
andreas.jakl@fh-hagenberg.at

Angelo Perkusich
Electrical Engineering Department
Electrical Engineering and Informatics Center
Federal University of Campina Grande
CP 10105
58109-970 Campina Grande, PB
Brazil
perkusic@dee.ufcg.edu.br

Kyller Costa Gorgônio
Signove Technology
58400-565 Campina Grande, PB
Brazil
kyller.gorgonio@signove.com

Hyggo Oliveira de Almeida
Computer Science Department
Electrical Engineering and Informatics Center
Federal University of Campina Grande
CP 10105
58109-970 Campina Grande, PB
Brazil
hyggo@dsc.ufcg.edu.br

Hassan Charaf
Budapest University of Technology and Economics
Magyar Tudósok körútja 2.
1117 Budapest
Hungary
hassan@aut.bme.hu

Bertalan Forstner
Budapest University of Technology and Economics
Applied Mobile Research Group
Magyar Tudósok körútja 2.
1117 Budapest
Hungary
bertalan.forstner@aut.bme.hu

András Berke
Budapest University of Technology and Economics
Applied Mobile Research Group
Magyar Tudósok körútja 2.
1117 Budapest
Hungary
andras.berke@aut.bme.hu

Imre Kelényi
Budapest University of Technology and Economics
Applied Mobile Research Group
Magyar Tudósok körútja 2.
1117 Budapest
Hungary
Imre.Kelenyi@aut.bme.h

FOREWORD

The world is full of programming languages and development tools. Some languages can be designed for embedded devices, others for ease of development. Each of them has its own distinct syntax and its own distinct tools, and is suitable for a distinct purpose. This has been a dilemma for a long time, especially in the mobile arena. Companies have their own development tools, programming paradigms and selected programming languages, and the same code can rarely be reused between different segments, from mobile terminals to desktop environments. Since the beginning of this century, Nokia has had three active software platforms: S60 (Symbian), S40 (proprietary) and Maemo (Linux). Each of these platforms has its own set of software components and applications. No matter what the application was, whether for a calculator or browser, Nokia had at least three different solutions for it. Each of these applications needed its own localization, tools and testing teams. Thus, it was self-evident that the overall development model was very expensive How then could this be reduced? How could a development model be created that the developers would love? How could a better return on software investments be provided? How could open source innovations be leveraged? The answer to this last question is very simple, but hard to actualize. First, you just create an environment or system where you can share code or applications between software platforms and then you do not implement everything from scratch, but leverage open source innovations. The implementation plan was also very simple: port the standard C programming libraries to S60, then find a common application development framework for S60 and Maemo and, lastly, provide a standard and common way to access platform-level services in the mobile domain. The work for Open C started in the first half of 2005. Most open source middleware solutions are developed on top of standard so-called C programming libraries: good old POSIX and other key C libraries. All together we ported 5000 C-function calls to S60. The commercial name was S60 Open C. Key libraries like libm, libc and libpthreads were delivered to Symbian Ltd. These are known as PIPS (Posix In Symbian). The next step was to find a good solution for an application UI development. The starting point was quite complex. Nokia Maemo was based on a GTK+ platform, S60 relied on Symbian AVKON and S40 had its own proprietary UI library. The whole of 2007 was spent on figuring out the right path to follow to go forward. The end result was that Nokia selected Qt as the next application development framework. Qt was also well known for its consistent, stable, robust and high-quality APIs and world-class documentation, but the most important thing was that developers loved Qt. As one software engineer stated: 'Qt gave the joy of programming back to me!' The way Qt was created, the cleanliness of the APIs and architecture, and the involvement of talented people created a good starting point. Qt is a powerful technology providing a great performance, a product loved by developers, an open source development model and a way of mixing web and native technologies. Thus, in January 2008, Nokia tendered a public offer to acquire Trolltech ASA. The announcement stated for the first time the role of Qt and Open C as part of Nokia's software strategy:

> The acquisition of Trolltech will enable Nokia to accelerate its cross-platform software strategy for mobile devices and desktop applications, and develop its Internet services business. With Trolltech, Nokia and third party developers will be able to develop applications that work in the Internet, across Nokia's device portfolio and on PCs. Nokia's software strategy for devices is based on cross-platform development environments, layers of software that run across operating systems, enabling the development of applications across the Nokia device range. Examples of current cross-platform layers are Web runtime, Flash, Java and Open C.

The year 2008 was quite busy. Together with the 'Trolls', we at Nokia started the R&D integration project. Together we planned the missing pieces, such as support for multitouch and a common way to access mobile platform-level services, like bearer management. Today this is known as the Mobility API. This book is about how to develop Qt applications for Symbian. However, I would like to encourage developers to develop applications which can be shared between platforms. Qt is a cross-platform development framework. The same source code can be shared between Linux, Mac and Windows-hosted PCs and now also with Symbian. Why not make full use of the benefits of Qt? Just download the latest Qt Creator from the Web and with this book start your journey!

Mika Rytkönen
mika.rytkonen@nokia.com
Helsinki, December, 2009

PREFACE

*The function of good software is to make
the complex appear to be simple.*

Grady Booch

Motivation for the Book

The main reason why the editors started this book project is based on the fact that Qt on Symbian will be one of the most important steps in mobile development for years. Qt for Symbian will enable developers to create appealing mobile applications in a fast and efficient way. Qt has proven its strength for application developers for decades, while Symbian offers the most flexible mobile platform due to its openness for a wide range of APIs. Furthermore, Qt will provide cross-platform capabilities that allow porting of applications over a wide range of mobile devices. Even though the main focus is on Symbian devices, part of the code presented in the book can be ported to Nokia's Maemo platform or Windows Mobile devices.

Scope of the Book

To make it clear from the outset, this book does not serve as a compendium either for Qt or for Symbian development. The main scope of this book is to explain to the reader how Qt applications can be created in an easy and efficient way on Symbian devices. The reader will be made familiar with how to install the development environment and use it. Additionally, the book explains in detail the Symbian support available for Qt development in terms of APIs and the possibility to extend Qt applications with native Symbian. Throughout the book the authors link the reader to the appropriate sources, such as web pages or books.

Targeted Readership

The book is structured to be useful for beginners and professionals in the field of mobile device development. The book can be used for self-study as well as lecture notes for basic courses. It has seven chapters. As given below in Figure 1, we expect our readership to fall into three main groups: namely, total beginners, Symbian experts (but not familiar with Qt) and Qt experts (but not

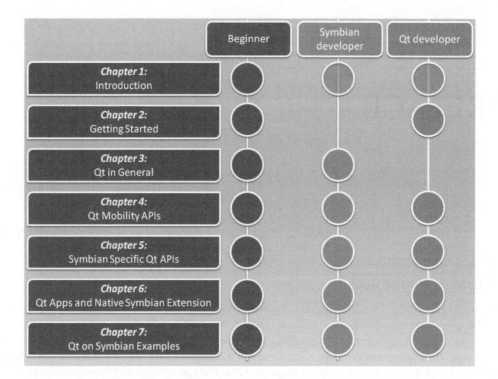

Figure 1 The book's structure and parts that should be read (marked by a bullet) by beginners, Symbian or Qt developers.

familiar with Symbian). Beginners should read the book chapter by chapter, while Symbian and Qt developers may skip Chapter 2 and Chapter 3, respectively. These latter two may also skip the Introduction. For teachers planning to use the book as their main lecture material throughout a course, we would like to direct them to our complementary web pages, where teaching slides, exercises and programming examples are presented.

`http://mobiledevices.kom.aau.dk/qt4symbian`

Note

Snippets of code included in the book are to some extent based on documentation available at the time of writing, and some of them have not been fully tested in real applications due to the relative freshness of the available implementations. The reader is referred to the latest available web documentation for exact details.

Frank H.P. Fitzek, Tony Torp and Tommi Mikkonen
December 2009

ABBREVIATIONS

3G Third Generation

API Application Programming Interface

ASCII American Standard Code for Information Interchange

DOM Document Object Model

DLL Dynamic Link Library

FM Frequency Modulation

FP Feature Pack

FTP File Transfer Protocol

GB Gigabyte

GPL GNU General Public Licence

GPS Global Positioning System

GUI Graphical User Interface

HTTP Hypertext Transfer Protocol

IDE Integrated Development Environment

IM Instant Messaging

IP Internet Protocol

IRDA Infrared Data Association

JRE Java Runtime Environment

LGPL Lesser GNU Public Licence

MHz Megahertz

MMS Multimedia Messaging Service

MOAP Mobile Oriented Applications Platform

OEM Original Equipment Manufacturer

OS Operating System

PC Personal Computer

RAM Random Access Memory

ROM Read-Only Memory

S60 Series 60

SAX Simple API for XML

SDK Software Development Kit

SIM Subscriber Identity Module

SMS Short Messaging Service

SQL Standard Query Language

STL Standard Template Library

SVG Scalable Vector Graphics

TCP Transmission Control Protocol

UDP User Datagram Protocol

UI User Interface

UIQ User Interface Quartz

URL Uniform Resource Locator

USB Universal Serial Bus

W3C World Wide Web Consortium

WLAN Wireless Local Area Network

XHTML Extensible Hypertext Markup Language

XML Extensible Markup Language

ACKNOWLEDGMENTS

*The man who can make hard things easy
is the educator.*

Ralph Waldo Emerson

This book is the result of the joint efforts of many people working together over the last few years. You would not be reading this book were it not for the key contributions of our invited authors as well as the kind support of Nokia and Qt software. We are deeply grateful to all our co-authors and industry (or 'other') supporters of this book.

We would like to thank Harri Pennanen and Jarmo Rintamaki from Nokia for encouraging us to start this book project. They have successfully kept up our motivation and enthusiasm over the last few months. Besides the material support provided, we greatly appreciate their logistical help by organizing numerous meetings to bring us together with other experts and programmers.

We are also greatly beholden to Knut Yrvin from Trolltech/Qt software. He encouraged us to incorporate Qt into our teaching environment and supported us with material such as the very first Greenphone and with travel funds over the years.

We are particularly thankful to Birgit Gruber, Chris Webb, Colleen Goldring, Ellie Scott, Graham Henry, Juliet Booker and Martin Tribe from Wiley for their help on the book.

The work of Aalborg University has been supported by the Danish government on behalf of the FTP activities within the CONE Project (grant no. 09-066549). The work of Federal University of Campina Grande, Campina Grande, Brazil, has been partially supported by the Nokia Institute of Technology, Manaus, Brazil, within the scope of the Pervasive Computing Project. We would also like to thank Flavio Fabrício Ventura de Melo Ferreira, from Federal University of Campina Grande.

Frank H.P. Fitzek, Tony Torp and Tommi Mikkonen
December 2009

PUBLISHER'S ACKNOWLEDGMENTS

Some of the people who helped bring this book to market include the following:

Editorial and Production:
VP Consumer and Technology Publishing Director: Michelle Leete
Associate Director – Book Content Management: Martin Tribe
Associate Publisher: Chris Webb
Executive Commissioning Editor: Birgit Gruber
Assistant Editor: Colleen Goldring
Publishing Assistant: Ellie Scott
Project Editor: Juliet Booker
Content Editor: Nicole Burnett
Copy Editor: Neville Hankins
Technical Reviewer: Antti Svenn

Marketing:
Senior Marketing Manager: Louise Breinholt
Marketing Executive: Kate Batchelor

Composition Services:
Compositor: Sunrise Setting Ltd, Torquay, UK
Indexer: Annette Musker

ABOUT THE EDITORS

Frank H.P. Fitzek is an Associate Professor in the Department of Electronic Systems, University of Aalborg, Denmark, heading the Mobile Device group. He received his diploma (Dipl.-Ing.) degree in Electrical Engineering from the University of Technology – Rheinisch-Westfälische Technische Hochschule (RWTH) – Aachen, Germany, in 1997 and his Ph.D. (Dr.-Ing.) in Electrical Engineering from the Technical University Berlin, Germany in 2002 and became Adjunct Professor at the University of Ferrara, Italy. He co-founded the start-up company acticom GmbH in Berlin in 1999. He has visited various research institutes including Massachusetts Institute of Technology (MIT), VTT, and Arizona State University. In 2005, he won the YRP award for the work on MIMO MDC and received the Young Elite Researcher Award of Denmark. He was selected to receive the NOKIA Champion Award in 2007, 2008 and 2009. In 2008, he was awarded the Nokia Achievement Award for his work on cooperative networks. His current research interests are in the areas of wireless and mobile communication networks, mobile phone programming, cross layer as well as energy-efficient protocol design and cooperative networking.

Tommi Mikkonen is a professor at Department of Software Systems at Tampere University of Technology. He has held several different positions in academia and industry, and at present his research interests include mobile devices programming, web development and agile approaches to software engineering. He is a well-known author and he has pioneered mobile devices programming in universities in Finland.

Tony Torp is a senior lecturer of software engineering at Tampere University of Applied Sciences where he is heading mobile systems education and running the smartphone lab of the University. He has a strong software development background in the industry since the very first Symbian based smartphone projects in Nokia. During the past decade he has shared his knowledge among several Universities, companies and developer communities worldwide. Being one of the top developers in the field, he received the Nokia Champion Award in 2006, 2009 and 2010. He is also running a company offering training and consultancy services for mobile developers.

1

Introduction and Motivation

Frank H.P. Fitzek, Tony Torp and Tommi Mikkonen

This chapter gives a short introduction to and motivation for the bundling of Qt and the Symbian platform. It will underline the importance of mobile developers in the mobile communication ecosystem and why they should choose Qt for Symbian. The chapter also explains the reasoning why Qt for Symbian is an interesting solution for a wide range of mobile developers – from rookies to experts – using the full functionality of the Symbian platform and enjoying the easy programming style of Qt in combination with its cross-platform capabilities.

1.1 The Importance of Mobile Developers

It was at end of the 1990s when mobile phones had become so popular that the question was posed: what will come after mobile voice services? At this time, only a small number of mobile phones were programmable and so it was up to the network and service operators to think about the next killer application – a reflection of the misunderstanding that a single application could attract as much attention as was gained previously by the mobile voice service. It took a while to appreciate that, not a single application, but a large number of heterogeneous applications, such as gaming, utilities, health services and others, would be the only viable solution to attract more customers. Furthermore, there was a common understanding across mobile manufacturers that the creators of the new and appealing services might not just be the network or service operators in collaboration with the mobile manufacturers, but that most of the services could be created by the mobile user. Or, since not all mobile users might be able to program, at least a subset of them should be able to create those services. We refer to this subset as mobile developers.

The reason why mobile manufacturers are so interested in increasing their developer base is due to the fact that the differences in mobile devices across different manufacturers are more in the design, user interaction as well as user friendliness, and the available services on board, than in the pure technology. Consequently, the manufacturers will take care of the design and a basic set of the most desired mobile applications, and the additional services will be provided by the developers. In order to enable customers to install new applications on their devices, new channels are provided to promote and market those additional mobile applications, as Nokia is doing with OVI, Apple with the Apple Store, and as RIM, SAMSUNG as well as Google plan to do in the near future.

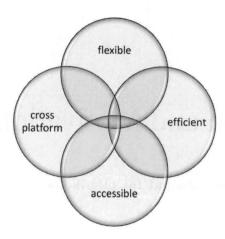

Figure 1.1 Developer needs.

Such marketplaces are important to allow the user of a mobile phone to install those applications that are needed and for mobile developers to monetize their work.

Mobile developers have several programming languages and platforms to program for. The problem is how to provide a programming environment that is easy for mobile developers to access (accessible), that has enough flexibility to utilize the full functionality of the mobile phone (flexible) and that allows the produced code to run efficiently on the platform (efficient). At the moment there is a clear trade-off between accessibility (how fast a developer can learn a language) and functionality and efficiency (what the platform readily offers). From the developer's point of view, there is a further problem when one aims at the mass market. If you want to reach a lot of users, the number of supported mobile phones should be large. Nowadays, independent of the programming environment, mobile applications need to be tailored for individual phones or groups of phones. This is true even for Java, which claims, once coded, to run everywhere. At the moment Java applications need to be tested on every single mobile phone to make sure they are working. As this costs time, it is desirable to have a cross-platform approach which would reduce the time wasted by testing for different devices. Therefore, as given in Figure 1.1, the desired programming environment should be flexible, accessible, efficient and at the same time cross-platform supportive.

From the perspective of mobile developers, the introduction of programmable mobile phones meant that the door was open for them to come up with services they always wanted to have or which they believed the mass market would like to purchase. The very first mobile applications were in the gaming area, and they were based on Java. Consequently, they were subject to the restrictions of the early versions of mobile Java, which in essence only provided a sand-box on which applications could be run and a very limited set of interfaces. Due to the given limitations, not all the functionalities of mobile phones could be used. For instance, since personal data of the user could not be accessed in early mobile Java implementations for security reasons, the first applications were stand-alone applications that could easily be executed in a sand-box, such as games or utilities like calendars or address books, which needed no connection to the functions of the rest of the phone.

With the introduction of the Symbian platform and its programming language Symbian C++, a larger degree of freedom became available to developers because more functionality of the phones could be used. The new degrees of freedom allowed the construction of mobile applications that, for example, used short-range technologies such as IRDA or Bluetooth to exchange data among mobile devices, or interfaced with the built-in facilities of the phone. One of the very first applications was a dating client that checked for matching user profiles, resulting in a notification in the case of a positive match. Also, IP network connections using the cellular operators' network were possible. Besides these, Symbian also had the technological advantage of using native code. Thus applications built with Symbian C++ consumed less resources and ran faster than other solutions at that time.

On the downside, however, Symbian C++ has one big disadvantage over many other programming languages and systems. Being a C++ derivative extended with proprietary conventions and a somewhat complex application framework resulted in difficulties in its adoption by a large number of mobile developers. Consequently, since the learning curve of Symbian C++ is rather steep, the number of real Symbian C++ developers is quite low compared with, say, Java developers. A number of attempts have therefore been made to support mobile developers in approaching Symbian.

To open up the Symbian platform to a larger group of developers, Nokia introduced Python for S60 (S60 is just a subset of the Symbian platform). Python for S60, released as open source at
http://opensource.nokia.com/projects/pythonfors60/
extends the S60 platform with the Python programming language. With the available infrastructure, developers are encouraged to undertake rapid application development and prototyping, and are provided with an option to create stand-alone S60 applications written in Python. Using the easy-to-learn Python scripting language, even people who have never programmed before are now able to write their own script and realize their own ideas. However, the Python interpreter is not readily available in off-the-shelf mobile devices but must be installed later on, which in turn results in additional installation tasks when using Python. This can be discouraging for some users, who want simply to experiment with rapidly available applications, not to install additional program infrastructure. Interested readers are referred to Scheible and Tuulos (2007) and Scheible (2010) for further information about Python for S60.

Another attempt to ease the developers' lot was Open C/C++ from Nokia (2010). Open C/C++ delivers an extensive range of standard C and C++ APIs. They are intended to help in porting desktop applications to Symbian devices. Moreover, they can also be helpful when developing application engines and middleware based on already existing components. In general, Open C/C++ enables the reuse of already existing software assets and open-source components. Instead of using a scripting language, Open C/C++ allows the use of real C or C++ code, which can be extended to phone-related libraries to employ those functionalities too. This approach has solved some of the problems associated with Symbian development, but there still remain demanding coding issues regarding the user interface.

The most recent step towards introducing Symbian programming to all mobile developers is the introduction of Qt for Symbian, which provides exactly those four essential features mentioned above – it is an accessible, flexible, cross-platform development environment for developing applications efficiently. The goal of the platform is to allow developers to target a large mobile developer group. The reason for the marriage of Qt with Symbian is based on the fact that Qt, as a cross-platform application framework, allows applications to be written once and deploys them across many operating systems without rewriting the source code. Furthermore, the underlying Symbian platform guarantees the highest possible flexibility in providing all the functionalities of a mobile phone. Qt development is done in C++. Moreover, Qt APIs have been designed with cross-platform use in mind, and are commonly considered easy to learn and use. The Qt APIs provide a higher level of abstraction than the Symbian APIs. From a developer's perspective the complexity of Symbian is hidden behind interfaces provided by Qt, which means that development becomes easier and developers get results much quicker. As a result, the authors of this book believe that it presents a timely topic and the following chapters should help developers to get started with Qt on the Symbian platform.

The rest of this chapter offers a short introduction to Symbian and Qt, including their philosophy in particular. We do not claim completeness for the individual parts. The idea is to create a common understand among all readers for both technologies. For further reading we will provide links to other work.

1.2   Symbian OS

Symbian OS is a leading-edge mobile development platform used in widely deployed mobile phones. Relying on C++, a microkernel, and extensive use of object-oriented design, it has enabled the development of a number of devices and given birth to Symbian, the most widely used platform in today's smart phones. The origins of Symbian OS can be traced back to the 1990s and Psion mobile devices. Being the state of the art at the time, Psion's devices were modest in terms of performance and capabilities by today's standards, and the ability of Symbian OS to support the introduction of new features expected of mobile phones can be taken as a tribute to the original designers. The path from the operating system of Psion devices to the Symbian platform – the most prominent Symbian environment in use today – has passed through numerous phases, from its origins at Psion to the newly created Symbian Foundation.

The origins of Symbian OS lie in the designs of Psion PLC, and include in particular SIBO, or EPOC16, which was based on C, and later EPOC32, which was to be named Symbian in its later life. The company was also developing associated software development kits to enable third-party application development, something which turned out to be important when the next steps towards the current smart-phone platform were taken.

The company Symbian, the original home base of Symbian OS as we know it today, was established in 1998 to develop a mobile platform for smart phones. Originally owned by a number of major mobile device companies – Ericsson, Matsushita, Motorola, Nokia and Psion – the goal was to license Symbian OS to the manufacturers of advanced 2.5G and 3G mobile phones, with much of the intellectual property originating from Psion PLC. The development mode was such that the company Symbian focused on the core operating system and main frameworks, whereas licensees developed different device-specific variations, including Symbian for phone-like devices, at least originally, and UIQ for communicators relying on a touchscreen.

The creation of the Symbian Foundation was announced on 24 June 2008 by major names in the mobile industry, including Nokia, Sony Ericsson, Motorola and NTT DOCOMO. The goal of the foundation is to create the most proven, open and complete mobile software platform in the world. In terms of technology, the aim is to unify Symbian OS, S60, UIQ and MOAP(S) in an open-source platform for converged mobile devices.

1.2.1   Symbian – The Technology

The design decisions of Symbian OS closely reflect its origins addressed above. It is an operating system that is specifically targeted for systems with limited memory and resources in general, following the state-of-the art design from the 1990s. The most characteristic design decisions are as follows.

Symbian OS is based on the microkernel architecture. The term microkernel is commonly associated with a design where all resource managers that have access to the underlying hardware run in different processes and the operating system kernel only has minimal scheduling and interrupt handling responsibility. Moreover, it is common for the microkernel to implement a message-passing mechanism which allows resource managers to communicate using the facilities that the kernel provides. In the design of Symbian OS, the introduction of a microkernel has been an important goal.

The use of the microkernel approach has resulted in the definition of special software components, whose purpose is to manage different types of resources. As is common in microkernel approaches, such resource managers are referred to as servers. Every resource of the system is encapsulated into a server, which is responsible for managing the resource. When the resource is used, the client first contacts the server, and then establishes a session with the server. After establishing the session, the client can use the resources and services offered by the server. Also, error management is incorporated into the scheme. If a server is killed, error messages are passed to the clients, and if a client dies, the server should be able to release the allocated resources.

The design of Symbian OS is based extensively on object orientation. A number of extensive frameworks are used for different tasks, including application development (application framework) and generic event handling (active objects), both of which will be addressed in the following. The latter is also associated with resource management, as servers – that is, resource managers – communicate with their clients using messages, the reception of which results in the generation of an event. Moreover, since programming facilities for C++, the language used for implementing the majority of Symbian OS, were underdeveloped at the time of the design, numerous proprietary conventions were introduced to cope with corner cases. Over time, the improvement of off-the-shelf C++ systems has in principle rendered some of these conventions useless, but their removal from the actual code base can be hard.

1.2.2   Symbian – Evolution to the Leading Smart-Phone Platform

As with any long-lived operating system, assumptions about available hardware have required redesign and reconsideration of numerous parts of Symbian OS. Since the main context of Symbian OS is smart phones, it is only natural that the evolution of their assumed facilities has also been the driving force of Symbian OS evolution. Major changes in Symbian OS include at least the following issues.

Hardware facilities have changed fundamentally. The original Psion devices relied on RAM disks that were fast but required a separate backup during writes. However, mobile devices commonly use flash memory for implementing disks. Due to the physical characteristics of flash memory, a new file is required in any case.

The amount of memory in different mobile devices has increased tremendously. Indeed, it is not uncommon to find hundreds of megabytes of available memory and gigabytes of disk, which were major improvements in the state of the art in the early 2000s when the first Symbian-based mobile phones were introduced. Consequently, many considerations regarding the use of memory that were a necessity in early mobile phones using Symbian OS are no longer needed, especially when considering the tasks of an application programmer. For a device manufacturer, however, these issues remain valid.

In parallel with the increase in the amount of memory, processing capabilities have improved. In addition to the increase in clock frequency, more and more processing-capable peripherals have been introduced. In general, Symbian's microkernel-based approach is well suited for this, but different extensions obviously require engineering efforts to integrate them into complete Symbian-OS-based systems.

The number of different subsystems that can be attached to current mobile phones has increased. At the same time, individual subsystems have become increasingly complex. As a consequence, their cumulative effect in incorporating support for all of them has added to the complexity of Symbian OS. For example, the adaptation interface between Symbian OS and underlying hardware resources which originally consisted of only a few servers has grown into a complex framework, where a plug-in architecture is used for variability between different hardware components.

The introduction of platform security has required a major redesign of Symbian OS. Consequently, this phase also marks a major disruption in the evolution of Symbian OS. For an application developer, this also marks a major breach in the compatibility between different devices in general, not to mention binary compatibility, which was also breached.

Symbian OS's ability to sustain the above is a tribute to the original design that still forms the core of the operating system. In particular, the microkernel architecture has proven to be a flexible platform for complex applications, and embedding resources in servers has provided a practical approach for managing the ever-increasing number of new resources associated with mobile phones. On the downside, the evolution of the platform has led to complications that are visible to a casual developer, especially in the form of evolving documentation.

1.2.3   Symbian – Casual Application Developer

While the facilities of Symbian OS have been improving under the hood, for a casual programmer Symbian OS's facilities have remained somewhat challenging. The challenges can be associated with two particular design choices: the Symbian application architecture, which is to be used as the basis for developing applications with a graphical user interface (GUI); and a number of platform-specific details, which can be considered as superfluous complexities by an application developer. This is considered frustrating when the development of applications for Symbian OS is performed only occasionally. Besides Python and Open C/C++, Qt for Symbian is an interesting solution. Qt is a cross-platform application development framework that is widely used for the development of GUI programs. Although commonly associated with GUI programming, the system also includes numerous other components, such as threading and interfacing to subsystems such as SQL database and XML parsing. Internally Qt is based on C++, but it includes several non-standard extensions implemented by an additional preprocessor, which, however, generates standard C++ code. Qt runs on all major platforms and supports internationalization.

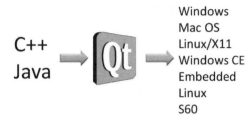

Figure 1.2 Qt development process: program once and use multiple platforms.

1.3   Qt

Qt (pronounced cute) is a product of QtSoftware which was originally named Trolltech (founded in 1994). Based on the initial idea of creating an object-oriented presentation system, the very first prototype was ready in 1993, and Trolltech was founded one year later in Norway. On 20 May 1995, the first public release was launched under the name Qt 0.9. The name was a result of the nice-looking letter Q in the Harvard Emacs editor and the Xt technology, see Yrvin (2010). Over the last few years Qt has been used by many customers such as Google, Skype, Volvo and many more.

1.3.1   A Cross-platform Development Environment

The main idea behind Qt was the possibility to program an application in C++ or Java once and deploy it across many desktop and embedded operating systems without changing the code at all (see Figure 1.2). From the developers' point of view the supported Qt APIs remain the same across the supported platforms, provided that the developers are using common APIs only and do not use device-specific interfaces, such as those offered in mobile devices only. Moreover, the same toolchain is available for different computing systems to support similar development experiences, which in turn results in increased productivity over different toolchains targeted for different contexts.

In addition to the same APIs, when using Qt the resulting applications should look like a native program of the given platform to ensure user friendliness – namely, adaptive look and feel. Figure 1.3 shows the look of Qt buttons for multiple platforms. In contrast to Java's SWING module where the application would also possibly run on all different platforms, the user interface would always look the same, which could cause some irritation to the customer who is used to a given handling of the applications. Qt comes with an intuitive class library and integrated development tools offering support for C++ and Java development. In addition to APIs and cross-compilation support, and in some cases more importantly, tools supporting Qt development were introduced, such as Qt Designer or Qt Linguist.

1.3.2   Qt in the Mobile Domain

In the beginning Qt was targeted at Windows, Mac OS (starting with Qt 3.0) and Linux systems only. However, the approach was so appealing that it was quickly expended to embedded systems in 2000. Finally, in 2006 Trolltech introduced the Greenphone, which is a fully featured mobile phone based

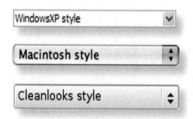

Figure 1.3 Qt look and feel for multiple platforms.

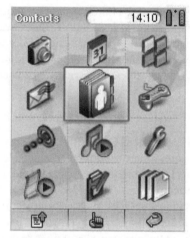

(a) The Greenphone   (b) User interface of the Greenphone

Figure 1.4 The very first Qt mobile phone.

on Linux (see Figure 1.4a). The Greenphone already had a touchscreen and a number of wireless air interfaces. Figure 1.4b shows the user interface of the Greenphone.

In 2008 Nokia took over Trolltech and introduced Qt to its platforms starting with the Symbian and Linux platforms. Together with the technology Nokia achieved access to a large and agile programming community. But as this is a two-way street, Qt programmers can now access the mobile domain with millions of new target devices yearly. In addition to the existing programming languages of Java, Symbian C++, Python or Flash, the introduction of Qt and its toolchain to mobile devices will reduce the number of hurdles to creating a mobile application.

The vision of Qt has been to introduce it everywhere – covering both the desktop and the mobile domain. In the mobile domain Qt is available on Linux-enabled devices and Nokia has pushed Qt onto the Symbian platform. In order to enable Qt to use the full range of mobile functionalities, such

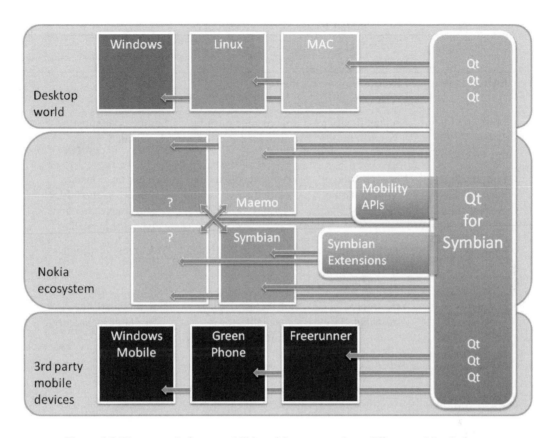

Figure 1.5 The cross-platform capabilities of Qt source code on different mobile platforms.

as those that are not available in the desktop world, new Symbian APIs need to be introduced. These APIs are responsible for using localization information, mobile messaging such as SMS and MMS, cameras, inbuilt sensors and many more things. Of course it is possible to create mobile applications for the Symbian platform without using the newly introduced APIs, but obviously those APIs have the potential to create real mobile applications for location-based services, social mobile networks and many others.

Figure 1.5 illustrates the applicability of Qt software for different platforms. As long as pure Qt language is used, the code should work on any platform, including desktops and laptops, Nokia ecosystems and third-party mobile devices. On the other hand, Symbian APIs can only be used for the Symbian platform and may be extendable later for other platforms of the Nokia ecosystem. Such an approach is similar to the Qt embedded approach, where functionalities such as phone-related access of calendars and contacts or the use of wireless short-range Bluetooth are limited to the embedded environment.

Table 1.1   License Agreements of Qt.

	Commercial version	LGPL version	GPL version
Licence cost	Licence fee charged	Free	Free
Must provide source code changes to Qt	No, modifications can be closed	Source code must be provided	Source code must be provided
Can create proprietary applications	Yes – no source code must be disclosed	Yes, in accordance with the LGPL v2.1 terms	No, applications are subject to the GPL and source code must be made available
Updates provided	Yes, to those with valid maintenance	Yes, freely distributed	Yes, freely distributed
Support	Yes, freely distributed	Not included but available for purchase separately	Not included but available separately for purchase
Charge for runtimes	Yes	No	No

1.3.3   Qt Licensing

The most important issue for mobile developers is the licence agreement. Qt is offering different licence models. While the commercial and GPL versions have been present from the beginning, the LGPL has only been added recently. The latter allows developers to monetize their applications without making their source codes public. Qt is available under the following licences:

Qt Commercial Version This version is the appropriate one to use for the development of proprietary and/or commercial software. It is for developers who do not want to share the source code with others or otherwise comply with the terms of the GNU Lesser General Public Licence version 2.1 or GNU GPL version 3.0.

Qt GNU LGPL v2.1 This version of Qt is appropriate for the development of Qt applications (proprietary or open source) provided developers can comply with the terms and conditions contained in GNU LGPL version 2.1.

Qt GNU GPL v3.0 This version of Qt is appropriate for the development of Qt applications where developers wish to use such applications in combination with software subject to the terms of GNU GPL version 3.0 or are otherwise willing to comply with the terms of GNU GPL version 3.0.

In Table 1.1 the licence agreements are compared with each other.

Bibliography

Nokia F 2010 Open C and C++. http://www.forum.nokia.com/Resources_and_Information/Explore/ Runtime_Platforms/Open_C_and_C++/.

Scheible J 2010 Python for S60 tutorials. http://www.mobilenin.com/pys60/menu.htm.

Scheible J and Tuulos V 2007 *Mobile Python: Rapid prototyping of applications on the mobile platform.* John Wiley & Sons, Inc.

Yrvin K 2010 Qt introduction. Oral Presentation Material.

2

Getting Started

Morten V. Pedersen, Janus Heide, Frank H.P. Fitzek and Tony Torp

This chapter gives an overview of the tools used for Qt development for the Symbian platform. The early sections will serve as an entry point for developers who are new to the Symbian platform by providing a step-by-step introduction and installation guide to the tools needed. The sections following will go through the process of creating and running a 'Hello World' application using Qt for Symbian both in the emulator and on a mobile phone. If you already have a working Symbian development environment and are familiar with the tools and application build process, it is recommended that you scan through the first part of the chapter as some SDK versions require patching or similar, before proceeding to Section 2.1.7 which focuses on the installation and introduction of the Qt for Symbian SDK. Note that throughout the chapter some long download links have been shortened using a URL shortener service. If a shortened link does not work, a table containing the original links can be found at the end of the chapter.

2.1 Installing the Development Environment

Figure 2.1 shows an overview of the components that comprise a typical Qt for Symbian development environment.

As indicated in the figure, the only currently supported development platform is Windows and it is recommended that users run either Windows XP or Windows Vista. This restriction is due to the fact that some tools in the Symbian platform SDK are only available on the Windows platform. There is, however, an ongoing effort to add official support for other development host environments, e.g. Linux or Mac, so this requirement will therefore most likely be removed in future versions of the Symbian platform SDK. In addition to the current Windows requirement, it is recommended that a reasonably fast development PC is used, i.e. an 1800 MHz processor, 2 GB RAM and enough free hard drive space for the tools, IDE and SDK. During the installation you will need to download approximately 1 GB of tools and updates. All tools take up approximately 2.3 GB installed. This installation process may take several hours depending on which components you install.

Assuming that we already have a working Windows development machine, the first tool we need to install and set up is a working Symbian development environment. Once this is installed we can extend it also to support Qt for Symbian development. In the following we will go through the installation of the individual components.

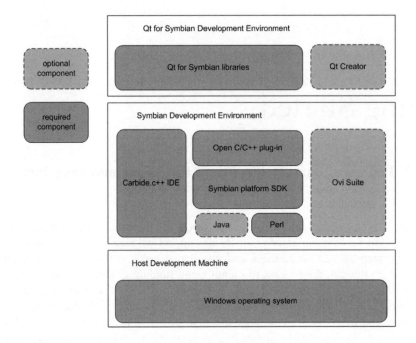

Figure 2.1 Overview of the tools comprising a Qt for Symbian development environment.

2.1.1   Ovi Suite

As shown in Figure 2.1, the Ovi Suite is an optional component. However, it is recommended that it is installed as it enables easy transfer and installation of applications to the phone. If you already have the Nokia PC Suite application installed, you may skip this installation, as the PC Suite software provides similar functionality. After installing the Ovi Suite you can connect your Symbian device to your development machine using either Bluetooth of a USB cable.

Download: `http://www.nokiausa.com/exploreservices/ovi/ovisuite`

2.1.2   Java

In order to utilize the phone emulator fully, a working installation of the Java Runtime Environment is necessary. The phone emulator is a valuable tool in the development and testing of our applications. Here you may install the latest available Java version. If you do not intend to use the device emulator, this step can be skipped. Note that installing a JRE above version 5 may cause the error 'Cannot start ECMT manager' to appear when trying to access the preferences of the Symbian emulator; to resolve this problem see: `http://bit.ly/7WCpIf`.

Download: `http://www.java.com/en/download/`

2.1.3 Perl

Several of the build scripts in the Symbian platform SDK rely on Perl. The officially supported version is ActiveState Perl version 5.6.1 build 635. During the installation of ActiveState Perl ensure that the 'Add Perl to the PATH environment variable' option is checked. Note that if you install a different version of Perl the Symbian build toolchain may not function properly.

Download: `http://bit.ly/4vOXGX`

> **Note:** The ActivePerl package should be installed before installing a Symbian SDK, otherwise the installation might fail.

2.1.4 Symbian Platform SDK

The Symbian platform SDK includes the documentation, compiler, headers, libraries and additional tools that are needed to build applications for a Symbian device. You will find that there are a number of different SDK versions, each targeting different Symbian platforms. Historically Symbian delivered the core operation system, which was then extended by different vendors using their own UI platforms. Of these the two most well-known UI platforms were the S60 platform used mainly by Nokia and the UIQ platform used mainly by Sony Ericsson and Motorola. However, since the Symbian Foundation was formed in 2008 these have now been merged into one platform maintained by the foundation. This change is so new that we still use the vendor-specific SDKs during development. The following table shows the platforms that currently support Qt for Symbian development:

Platform	Symbian OS version	Example devices
S60 3rd Edition Feature Pack 1	v9.2	5700, 6120, E63, E71, N82, N95
S60 3rd Edition Feature Pack 2	v9.3	5730, 6650, E55, E75, N85, N96
S60 5th Edition (Symbian^1)	v9.4	5800, N97

Note that in this table the first Symbian Foundation SDK (Symbian^1) is a copy of the S60 5th Edition SDK. However, future versions of the Symbian Foundation SDKs will replace vendor-specific SDKs. These will be named Symbian^2, Symbian^3, and so forth. When developing applications using native Symbian C++ APIs, you have to use an appropriate SDK determined by which version of the Symbian and UI platform your target device uses. This is, however, not necessary with Qt for Symbian, since with Qt we may use any of the mentioned SDKs for application development and deployment. Should you need to access features of the Symbian platform not yet available through the Qt libraries, you can determine which SDK you need, for a specific target device, in the device specification section on Forum Nokia (`http://www.forum.nokia.com/devices/`). Note that platforms prior to the 3rd Edition Feature Pack 1 do not support Qt for Symbian.

If you do not have a suitable device available, you may select any of the above-listed SDKs. Without a physical device you will still be able to test and run your applications in the device emulator. If you wish to target several different S60 platforms, it is perfectly acceptable to install several different SDKs.

> **Note:** If you choose to use Symbian C++ native code/extensions the different platform SDK versions are to some extent backward binary compatible. This means that applications built with, for example, a 3rd Edition SDK in most cases also run on a 5th Edition device. However, there are exceptions, so it is recommended to install multiple SDKs and build the application for each platform.

Installing the Symbian SDK

In order to download the SDK you will need a valid Forum Nokia account which can be obtained at `http://www.forum.nokia.com/Sign_Up.xhtml` free of charge. After completing the registration and logging in to the Forum Nokia website, you may download the SDK from the following location:

Download: `http://bit.ly/4qdgTk`

If you are installing the 3rd Edition Feature Pack 2 or 5th Edition SDK the installation files can be found by pressing the 'Download all-in-one S60 SDKs' button.

If you are installing the 3rd Edition Feature Pack 1 SDK you will find the installation files by pressing the 'Download S60 SDKs for C++' button.

After downloading, the installation can be completed in the following three steps:

1. The SDK is delivered in one zip file. Unzip the contents to a temporary directory.

2. Run the setup.exe file in the temporary directory.

3. Follow the installer, choose the default options, i.e. accept the licence agreement, choose a 'Typical' installation, and install the 'CSL ARM Toolchain'.

Patching the 3rd Edition Feature Pack 1 SDK

In order for Qt for Symbian to function properly with the 3rd Edition Feature Pack 1 SDK we need to apply one additional patch to the installation:

1. A new version of the getexports.exe file needs to copied to the `epoc32\tools` sub-directory, e.g. `C:\Symbian\9.2\S60_3rd_FP1\epos32\tools`. The updated getexports.exe file can be downloaded from: `http://bit.ly/8KMG9K`.

Overview of the Symbian SDK

This section provides a brief overview of the SDK and the contents, e.g. where to find Symbian-specific documentation. If you are installing more than one of the SDKs supported by Qt for Symbian and are using the default suggested installation paths, you will notice that the SDK root directory since 3rd Edition Feature Pack 2 is installed under `S60\devices\SDKversion` and older SDKs are installed under `Symbian\OSversion\SDKversion`. In addition, several SDK sub-folders have changed names. The following table gives an overview of selected folders in the SDKs and their contents:

3rdFP1 Edition	3rdFP2 and 5th Editions	Description
Epoc32	Epoc32	Contains cross-compiler, emulator and system headers and libraries
Examples	Examples	Non-S60 specific Symbian OS code examples
Series60Doc	docs	The SDK documentation files, including API descriptions
Series60Ex	S60CppExamples	Code examples, typically S60 platform specific
Series60Tools	S60tools	Development tools, e.g. SVG to SVG-T converter

The epoc32 folder containing the emulator also contains the drive mapping used when testing applications in the emulator. Note that on the target device the `z:` drive is used for the ROM and contains the operating system files and standard applications. The `c:` drive provides both memory for running processes and storage for new applications. During building for the emulator the drives are mapped into the following directories:

c: is mapped to `\epoc32\winscw\c`.

z: is mapped to `\epoc32\release\winscw\variant\z`.[1]

When building for the emulator, the build tools assume that we are building system applications and therefore place them in `z:`. However, files created while the application is running in the emulator will be placed in the `c:` directory. Another important folder is the documentation folder, which contains various help files. The SDK documentation can also be accessed via the Windows Start menu under 'S60 Developer Tools'. Here you will also find the Symbian Developer Library containing searchable guides and API documentation, see Figure 2.2. Later, when we create our first Qt for Symbian application, you will see a number of Symbian-specific files being generated; the purpose of these is described in the Symbian Developer Library. This library may also be accessed from the Carbide.c++ help menu.

2.1.5   Open C/C++ Plug-in

We now have the Symbian platform SDK installed and ready for use. However, the SDK does not include the Open C/C++ version 1.6 plug-in required by Qt for Symbian. The Open C/C++ plug-in provides developers with standard C and C++ libraries, e.g. support for the C++ Standard Library. We therefore have to install the plug-in into our installed Symbian SDK:

Download: `http://bit.ly/R1C2q`

---

[1] Variant refers to the build variant, and should be replaced with **udeb** for debug builds and **urel** for release builds.

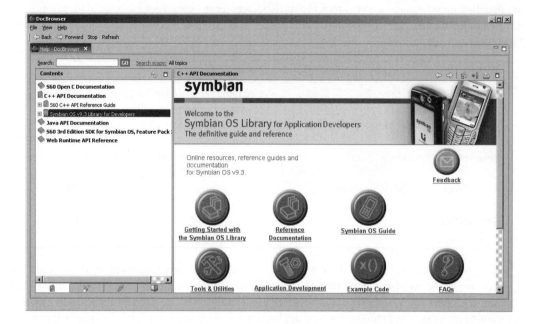

Figure 2.2 SDK documentation containing essential information about the Symbian APIs, Symbian OS architecture, development tools and programming idioms.

Installation of the Open C/C++ plug-in can be done in the following steps:

1. The plug-in is contained in a single zip file. Unzip the contents to a temporary folder.

2. Run the setup.exe file in the temporary directory.

3. The installer will automatically detect our installed SDKs. Select the SDKs that you wish to use for Qt development, and continue the installation, accepting any further default values.

4. The Open C/C++ libraries also need to be installed onto our target device. We will do this when installing the Qt for Symbian libraries.

Note: For new users it is recommended that all software is installed into the suggested default directories, as some applications have special requirements for the installation paths. Furthermore, if you have a default installation you can more easily find useful 'how-tos' and similar advice on the Internet.

Note: Both the Open C/C++ plug-in and the S60/Symbian SDK will require that you register your usage of them online. The Open C/C++ plug-in must be registered the first time you use it; the SDK, however, gives you a 14-day trail before requiring registration. The registration process is done via a registration wizard which requires that you can access your Forum Nokia web page account.

2.1.6   The Carbide.c++ IDE

The recommended IDE by Symbian and Nokia is currently the Eclipse-based Carbide.c++. The Carbide.c++ IDE provides support for creating, managing and building applications developed for the Symbian OS and S60 platform devices. Carbide.c++ is available for free in three different variants:

Variant	Features
Developer	Contains the tools needed to develop applications for S60/Symbian, including additional features such as on-device debugging
Pro	Extends the features of the Developer Edition with tools for performance analysis and extends the on-device debugging capabilities with system-level and crash debugging
OEM	Extends the features of the Pro version with tools needed by manufacturers when creating phones using Symbian OS

All three variants can be used for Qt for Symbian development, and all three are included in the Carbide.c++ installer which may be downloaded from Forum Nokia (you select your preferred version during the installation). The following steps will take you through the installation process:

Download: `http://bit.ly/6Rzaba`

1. Go to download URL and press the 'Download Carbide.c++' button.

2. Run the downloaded .exe file and choose the default options, i.e. accept the licence agreements, choose the Carbide.c++ variant to install and select the installation directory.

3. Currently the latest version of Carbide.c++ available from Forum Nokia's webpage is version 2.0. However, since Qt for Symbian currently requires Carbide.c++ version 2.0.2, you must perform an update, which is done from within the IDE. If this is your first time starting Carbide.c++ you will be prompted to select a *workspace* where Carbide.c++ will store new projects. If you have no specific reason to change it, select the default directory suggested by Carbide.c++. The update option can be found in *Help → Software Update → Find And Install*. As the update dialog appears, select *Search for update of the currently installed features* and click *Finish*. Once the update manager has found the updates available, you will be prompted to select an update mirror; if you are unsure which is the closest, select *Automatically select mirrors* and press *OK*. Select all updates and accept the licence agreement and the update process should start. Note that this process may take in excess of 20 minutes.

4. Qt for Symbian requires building projects to be enabled from the command prompt. This can be done by locating *Carbide.c++ → Configure environment for WINSCW command line* under the Windows Start menu.

> **Note:** If you are behind a proxy you will need to configure Carbide.c++ to use a proxy server:
>
> 1. From the menu bar select *Window → Preferences*.
> 2. Expand the *General* tab and select *Network Connections*. Select *Manual proxy configuration* and enter your proxy settings.

Patching the Carbide Compiler

To make the environment work properly we need to apply one patch to the Carbide.c++ installation; this is necessary as the Carbide compiler needs to be at least version 3.2.5, build 482 to be able to build Qt for Symbian properly. The compiler version number can be checked by executing the file mwccsym2.exe from the command line, e.g. `C:\ProgramFiles\Nokia\Carbide.c++v2.0\x86Build\Symbian_Tools\Command_Line_Tools\mwccsym2.exe`. If the compiler version is older than what was specified above, you should update your installation using the following steps:

1. A new version of the compiler needs to copied to the x86Build sub-directory of your Carbide.c++ installation, e.g. `C:\ProgramFiles\Nokia\Carbide.c++v2.0\x86Build`. The updated can be downloaded from: `http://bit.ly/5fQEj4`.

> **Note:** If you also plan to do native Symbian C++ programming the patch should not, but might, interfere with your Symbian builds. To ensure that you can always revoke the changes, you should create a backup of the x86Build directory before applying the patch.

After applying this last patch we now have completed the installation of the common tools used in a standard S60/Symbian development environment. In the following we install the Qt for Symbian libraries which will allow us to start developing Qt applications for our S60 devices.

2.1.7   Qt for Symbian

The latest version for Qt for Symbian is, at the time of writing, Qt 4.6; it contains the documentation, headers and libraries needed for Qt for Symbian development. This section will guide you through the installation:

Download: `http://qt.nokia.com/downloads`

1. Download the Qt for Symbian package from the URL above. On the download page you can choose which licence you wish to use – in this case choose the LGPL tab, which will show the available LGPL downloads. Here we select 'Qt libraries 4.6 for Symbian'.

2. The Qt for Symbian distribution is delivered in one .exe file. Download this .exe file to your hard drive and double-click it to start the installation.

3. The Qt installer will detect our installed Symbian SDKs and ask which one we want to use for Qt development. Here we can simply add support for all Symbian SDKs by selecting all the SDKs currently installed and pressing *Next*.

4. Then we have to choose the destination folder for the Qt libraries. Note that we must select a folder on the same drive as where we installed the Symbian SDK. Also, if you wish to use other versions of Qt, e.g. for Windows application development, you should change the destination folder to, say, `C:\Qt\4.6.0-symbian` to allow other Qt versions to be installed in the same folder.

Installing Qt on the Device

Before we can run Qt applications on our mobile device we need to install the Qt for Symbian libraries on to our device. This can be done in the following steps:

1. Uninstall any previously installed Qt or Open C/C++ libraries that may be on the device. This is done from the application manager found on the device.

2. Navigate to the Qt folder where we just installed the Qt libraries and tools (in our case, `C:\Qt\4.6.0-symbian`). In the folder locate the file called qt_installer.sis – this file contains the Qt libraries for the phone packed in a Symbian installation package (.sis file). Assuming you have installed the Ovi Suite and connected your mobile device through either USB or Bluetooth, you can now double-click the file and Ovi Suite will start the application installer on your device.

In the next step we need to set up Carbide.c++ to use the Qt for Symbian distribution.

Configuring Qt Support in Carbide.c++

Open Carbide.c++, go to *Window → Preferences* and select *Qt*. Under the Qt preferences click *Add* and in the *Add new Qt version* dialog enter the Qt version name, the path to the `bin` and `include` directories in the Qt installation folder as shown in Figure 2.3.

We are now ready to start building applications using Qt for Symbian.

2.2   Using Carbide.c++ with Qt for Symbian

This section provides an overview of the Carbide.c++ IDE. The first time you start Carbide.c++ you will be greeted with the Carbide.c++ welcome screen. The welcome screen contains a number of shortcuts to tutorials, release notes, etc. Specifically for Qt for Symbian, you may access *Overview → Qt Development*. The Qt development guide may also be accessed via *Help → Help Contents*. Development and project management are done in the workbench window, which can be accessed by pressing the *Workbench* icon in the top right corner of the welcome screen. You may revisit the welcome screen at a later stage by pressing *Help → Welcome*. The workbench window shown in Figure 2.4 can be broken down into the following main elements:

Project explorer This shows the folder structure of the current projects and allows for navigating the files.

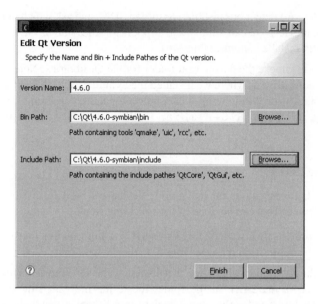

Figure 2.3 Qt properties must be updated in Carbide.c++.

Editor Used for viewing and editing source files.

Output window This window allows for several different views, e.g. the Problems view that display problems encountered during the build process of a project and the Console view which displays the output from the build process (compiler, linker, etc.).

Toolbar: Among other things this contains the 'Build' button which allows for building the current project, the 'Debug' button which launches the application in debug mode, and the 'Run' button which launches the application for functional testing.

This collection of views/windows is called a perspective in Carbide.c++ terminology. There are other useful perspectives such as the Debug perspective that contains the windows/views useful during a debug session, e.g. allowing for inspection of variables and breakpoints, and the Qt C++ perspective which we will use during Qt development. The perspective can be changed using the *Window → Open Perspective* menu item. If you switch to the Qt C++ perspective you will notice that some additional windows appear in the workbench, e.g. the Qt C++ Widget Box, the Qt C++ Property Editor and other Qt-related windows. We will use these in the following when working with new Qt for Symbian applications. Also in the following we will go through the basic steps of creating a 'Hello World' application using Qt for Symbian.

Creating a 'Hello World' Application

Now we can create our first project using the Carbide.c++ Project Wizard. The project wizard can be found under *File → New → Qt Project*. The application wizard will show the following available project templates for Qt projects:

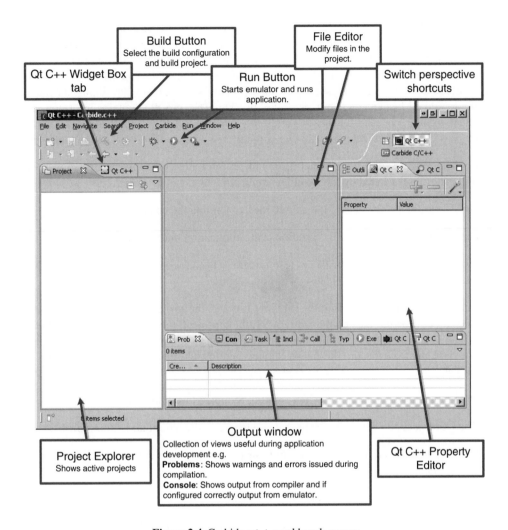

Figure 2.4 Carbide.c++ workbench screen.

Template	Purpose
Qt Console	Used for applications not requiring a GUI and provides the Qt event loop where network, timer events, etc., are processed
Qt GUI Dialog	Simple GUI application base on QDialog, which provides the basic functionality used in a dialog
Qt GUI Main Window	GUI application based on the QMainWindow class which provides a more sophisticated user interface option
Qt GUI Widget	Simple GUI application based on the QWidget class

Select the *Qt GUI Dialog* template and press *Next*. In the following dialog specify the name of the new Qt for Symbian project, in this case choose *helloworld*, and press *Next*. The application wizard will show a dialog containing a list of SDKs and build configurations that you can use for the project. The list depends on the SDKs installed; select the SDK you wish to use and press *Finish*. Carbide.c++ now creates the project and switches to the Qt C++ development perspective. Say 'OK' to adding headers and sources to the .pro file. The .pro file contains information about our application that is needed for the Qt build tools when building our application. In the *Project Explorer* view observe that the application wizard has created a number of files for the new project:

*_reg.rss The *_reg.rss file is a special Symbian resource file containing information about the application; it is needed by the Symbian application launcher or system shell.

.h/.cpp These are the standard C++ source files containing the code used in the project.

*.loc The .loc file can be used for localization if the application must support multiple languages.

*.rss A standard Symbian resource file. A resource file is used for defining a number of UI elements such as menus, dialogs, application icons and captions.

.inf/.mmp The component definition (bld.inf) file and the project definition (*.mmp) file are used to describe the files contained in a Symbian project; they are used, for example, when building the project from the command prompt. Using Qt for Symbian these files are generated automatically from the .pro file and we should therefore use the .pro file when changing project settings.

*.pkg A Symbian package file, used when creating Symbian installation files .sis.

*.pro The Qt project file, which serves the same purpose as the bld.inf and *.mmp files.

*.ui The Qt .ui file is used by the GUI design tools to describe the components and properties of a GUI application.

Makefile Automatically generated makefile for project compilation.

To edit one of the automatically generated files, double-click it and it will open in the Editor window. The project is now ready and we can build and run it in the emulator. However, since the application wizard created an empty project we should first add some functionality to the application. To add GUI components we may use the Qt Designer Editor. This can be done by double-clicking the .ui file, which should automatically open the design editor. To add a component switch to the Widget Editor view, press *Qt C++ Widget Box* in the upper left corner next to the *Project Explorer* tab. Select the Label widget and drag it to the Editor window. Changing the label text can be done by either right-clicking the label and selecting *Change plain text* or by selecting *Qt C++ Property Editor* and locating the text property for the label widget. Using the Property Editor we can manipulate a wide range of additional parameters controlling the appearance and functionality of the widgets. Change the label's text to 'helloworld', as shown in Figure 2.5.

To see how the application looks, build the project and run it in the S60 emulator by first pressing the 'Build' button to build the project and thereafter the 'Run' button as previously shown in

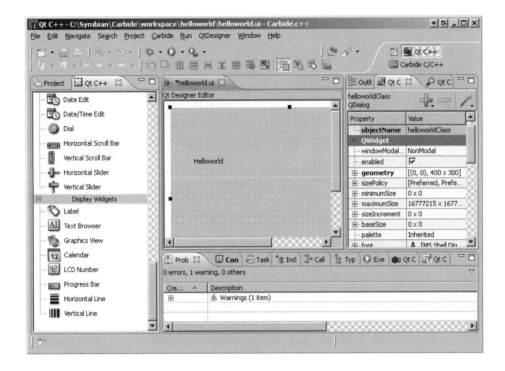

Figure 2.5 Using the Qt C++ perspective to design the UI of the application.

Figure 2.4. If all goes well you should see the emulator start and launch the application. This can take some time, so be patient.

> **Note:** If something unexpectedly does not work, you can find valuable information by inspecting the debugging output from the emulator. For the S60 3rd Edition this first needs to be enabled. There are two ways to achieve this: either edit the \epoc32\data\epoc.ini file where the line *LogToFile 0* must be changed to *LogToFile 1*, or control the same setting through the emulator's preferences menu. Select *Tools → Preferences* and choose the *Enable EPOCWIND.OUT logging* option. The log file named epocwind.out can be found in the Windows temporary directory, which may be accessed from the *Run* command in the Windows Start menu, by typing %temp%.

You can read more about using the emulator by searching for the keyword 'emulator' in the *Help → Help Contents* menu. Now that the application runs in the emulator we will configure the build process for a physical device.

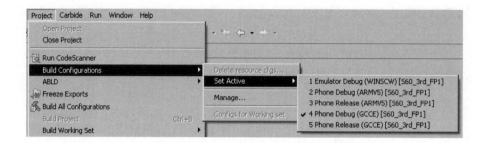

Figure 2.6 Selecting an active build configuration.

Building for a Target Device

In order to deploy the application on a phone we need to change the build configuration. This can be done in several ways, but we will do it by selecting the project from the *Project Explorer* tab and then using the *Project → Build Configuration → Set Active → Phone Debug (GCCE)* menu option. The new active build configuration is now marked as shown in Figure 2.6.

As when building for the emulator, we can use the *Project → Build Project* menu option, which will create a new file in *Project Explorer*, namely the helloworld_gcce_udeb.sisx (Symbian installation file). The easiest way to install the application on a phone is to use the Nokia Ovi Suite application installer and a Bluetooth dongle or USB cable. Make sure the Ovi Suite is connected to your phone and then simply double-click the .sisx file in the Project Explorer view so that the Ovi Suite application installer will be activated and allow you to begin the installation on the phone. Complete the installation on your phone. You should be able to find and run the application from the phone menu. Note that if Carbide.c++ does not build the .sisx file, we have to add the .pkg file to the SIS build property. This can be done through *Project → Properties → Build Configurations* and selecting the 'Phone Debug (GCCE)' configuration. Under the 'SIS Builder' tab add the .pkg file. You can leave all other options as they are. Press 'OK' to accept the changes and go to the Qt C++ perspective. Rebuild the project and the .sisx file should be created.

2.3   Summary

In this chapter we installed and tested our Qt for Symbian development environment. You should now be able to create new applications, run them in the emulator and on a physical device. The following table summarizes a number of good Internet resources where additional information or help may be obtained:

Forum Nokia Discussion Boards	http://discussion.forum.nokia.com
Forum Nokia Wiki	http://wiki.forum.nokia.com
Forum Nokia Developer's Library	http://library.forum.nokia.com/
Qt Developer Zone	http://qt.nokia.com/developer

Links

The following table shows the mapping or URLs used throughout the chapter:

Short URL	Original URL
`http://bit.ly/4qdgTk`	`http://www.forum.nokia.com/Resources_` `and_Information/Tools/Platforms/S60_` `Platform_SDKs/`
`http://bit.ly/7WCpIf`	`http://wiki.forum.nokia.com/index.` `php/KIS001066_-_'Cannot_start_ECMT_` `Manager'_error_message_in_emulator`
`http://bit.ly/4vOXGX`	`http://downloads.activestate.com/` `ActivePerl/Windows/5.6/`
`http://bit.ly/6Rzaba`	`http://www.forum.nokia.com/Resources_` `and_Information/Tools/IDEs/Carbide.` `c++/`
`http://bit.ly/R1C2q`	`http://www.forum.nokia.` `com/info/sw.nokia.com/id/` `91d89929-fb8c-4d66-bea0-227e42df9053/` `Open_C_SDK_Plug-In.html`
`http://bit.ly/5fQEj4`	`http://pepper.troll.no/` `s60prereleases/patches/x86Tools_` `3.2.5_Symbian_b482_qt.zip`
`http://bit.ly/8KMG9K`	`http://pepper.troll.no/` `s60prereleases/patches/getexports.` `exe`

In the following chapter the cross-platform Qt API is introduced, upon which most of our Qt for Symbian applications will be built.

3

Qt in General

Andreas Jakl

One of the major reasons for the success of Qt is that it is designed to be cross-platform. As a result, almost no in-depth knowledge is required about the specific platforms you want to target. The generic Qt code works everywhere; getting it on different platforms is just a matter of recompiling. Therefore, this chapter will introduce you to the general principles behind Qt. While not providing detailed in-depth explanations of every concept, the major areas are introduced to give you a quick overview of the way Qt works and how you can use it for your own purposes.

3.1 Hello World

In the previous chapter, you saw how to use the Qt Designer to create a user interface quickly. Now, we will take a look behind the scenes and develop the UI manually.

Of course, you could argue that it would be easier to use the Qt Designer instead of manually creating the necessary source code. While this argument is valid in many situations, it is still important to know how the user interface elements work, before outsourcing this task to the designer tool. Additionally, you will often have to modify or extend existing components to suit the exact needs of your application. This also requires directly working with the Qt classes.

As a first step, let us create the typical *Hello World* application. Of course, the aim of this application is to show the text 'Hello World' on the screen. See Figure 3.1 for a screenshot on Windows 7 and Symbian. Usually, you will use Qt Creator, Carbide.c++, Visual Studio or another IDE to create and manage your Qt projects. To understand how the multi-platform build chain works, let us do it manually this time.

First, create a file called `main.cpp` in an empty directory called `HelloWorld`. When working with the Symbian toolchain, make sure that the full path to your project directory does not contain any space characters and that it is on the same drive as the Symbian SDK.

```
1  #include <QApplication>
2  #include <QLabel>
3
4  int main(int argc, char *argv[])
5  {
6      QApplication app(argc, argv);
7      QLabel label("Hello World!");
```

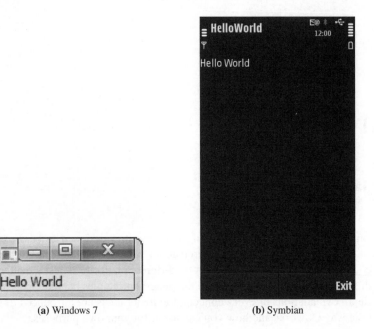

(a) Windows 7   (b) Symbian

Figure 3.1 The Hello World application, featuring a label with the famous piece of text.

```
8    label.show();
9    return app.exec();
10   }
```

The first two lines include the required header files for our application. As you can see by quickly scanning the source code, we use two classes, QApplication and QLabel. Conveniently, the corresponding header files have been given exactly the same name.

Next, the QApplication object is created. It takes care of managing application-wide resources and handles the main event loop. The command-line parameters are passed to the constructor, as Qt also supports some command-line arguments of its own.

Afterwards, we create a QLabel object with the text 'Hello World!' In Qt terms, this is called a widget, a visual element of the user interface. Initially, it is invisible. By calling its show() method, it will appear on the screen. As the label has no parent widget, it is automatically embedded in a window on the operating system's desktop.

In the last source code line, the exec() function passes control to Qt. The application enters its event loop and waits for user actions like mouse clicks, touch events or keyboard presses. If the user closes the application window, the exec() call returns and the application terminates.

3.1.1 Building

Now it is time to try the application. Open a command prompt, go to the directory where you have created your project and type:

```
qmake -project
```

This command generates a platform-independent project file (`HelloWorld.pro`), which contains information about the type of application to create (`app` or `lib`), the included source and header files (here, `main.cpp`) and other settings. If you get an error message, make sure the path to the `/bin/` folder of your Qt installation is part of the *PATH* system environment variable. The `.pro` file should look like this:

```
1  TEMPLATE = app
2  TARGET =
3  DEPENDPATH += .
4  INCLUDEPATH += .
5
6  # Input
7  SOURCES += main.cpp
```

Typing the following creates the platform-specific makefile from the project file. Depending on the target platform, different files will be created. On Symbian OS, this includes the resource file needed to show the application on the phone's menu and a Symbian-specific project file (`.mmp`):

```
qmake
```

The next step is to start the compiler for your current target platform. By default, `make` creates a release version. If you add the parameter `debug`, it accordingly creates a debug version. Use Carbide.c++ for on-device debugging on Symbian phones.

```
make
```

3.1.2   Packaging

In Windows, you can now directly start the `.exe` file and enjoy your 'Hello World' application. If you are using the Symbian SDK, there is one more step to go. Due to the security model on Symbian phones, you can no longer directly start `.exe` files. Instead, the system's installer component has to install all applications, so that it can check the validity of the certificate plus the requested permissions, and then copy the executable file into protected directories where hardly any other component has read/write access.

To package the application and to install it on your phone, first connect your phone to the PC and start the PC Suite. Then type:

```
createpackage -i HelloWorld_gcce_urel.pkg
```

This will package the executable and the generated resources files for the phone menu into an installable and self-signed `.sis` file. The `-i` parameter automatically installs it on the phone afterwards. Alternatively, you can use over-the-air delivery or simply send the `.sis` file to your phone via Bluetooth or a USB connection to install it manually. Follow the installation process on your phone to complete the installation.

3.2   Basics

A good way to start learning Qt is to work through an example. Initially, it demonstrates how to define the layout for multiple widgets and then deals with questions about memory management. Afterwards, the example is further expanded with a communication concept that dynamically connects multiple class instances.

3.2.1   Layouts

The previous section demonstrated the use of a single widget (called *control* in Symbian) as a window itself – essentially, it was made full screen on the Symbian device. In most situations, an application user interface is made of multiple widgets that are arranged on the screen according to some rules.

In Qt, this is done through various types of layout managers, which automatically align and resize the widgets they are in charge of. Managed layouts are especially important on mobile devices. A simple application on a desktop PC might very well have a fixed size that cannot be changed by the user – think of the simple calculator that comes with Windows. On the other hand, most mobile phones support screen rotation (e.g. using acceleration sensors). To maintain usability, applications typically have to adapt to the new screen orientation and scale the user interface on-the-fly. Consult the Qt documentation for a visual overview of the available layout managers.

The following example demonstrates the use of a vertical layout manager for three widgets – the resulting window is shown in Figure 3.2, for the platforms Windows 7 and Symbian:

```
1   #include <QApplication>
2   #include <QVBoxLayout>
3   #include <QSpinBox>
4   #include <QSlider>
5
6   int main(int argc, char *argv[])
7   {
8       QApplication app(argc, argv);
9       QWidget window;
10
11      QVBoxLayout* layout = new QVBoxLayout(&window);
12
13      QSpinBox* spinBox = new QSpinBox;
14      QSlider* slider = new QSlider(Qt::Horizontal);
15      QPushButton* exitButton = new QPushButton("Exit");
16
17      layout->addWidget(spinBox);
18      layout->addWidget(slider);
19      layout->addWidget(exitButton);
20
21      window.show();
22      return app.exec();
23  }
```

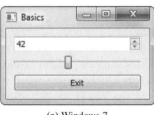

(a) Windows 7   (b) Symbian

Figure 3.2 A widget containing a spinbox, a slider and an exit button and using a vertical layout manager. (a) Application running on Windows 7. (b) Same application on Symbian.

The most obvious additions are three widgets – a slider, a spinbox and a push button – which are now arranged by the layout manager (`QVBoxLayout`). If we resize the window, the layout manager automatically makes sure that the widgets adapt to the available space. Of course, it is also possible to define the behaviour of widgets in more detail: for example, if you want the push button to stay sleek and small instead of occupying a large area of the screen. If developing native C++ code for Symbian, developers have manually to set positions and dimensions of all controls because no layout managers are available. For developers with previous experience in UIQ3, layout managers will be familiar.

In the previous section, we directly used the label widget as a window. This time, a simple `QWidget` class instance called `window` is created. `QWidget` is often use as a container for other widgets or sub-classed to create its own widgets. When it is constructed, no argument is supplied – this turns the object into the root of an object hierarchy (see Section 3.2.2). At the end of the `main()` method, the widget is turned into a window of its own through the `show()` method.

Next, the layout manager is created. The `QWidget` object is passed as an argument in the constructor to inform the `QVBoxLayout` that it is responsible for the layout of `window`.

The three widgets (`spinBox`, `slider` and `exitButton`) are constructed similarly to the label object in the first example. Both are added to the `QVBoxLayout`, which is going to manage those objects. As children of the window object, the three widgets automatically become visible when the parent object is shown on the screen. No extra calls of the `show()` method are necessary.

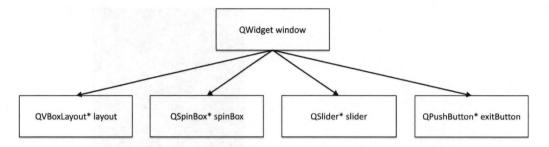

Figure 3.3 Classes inherited from QObject can be stored in a tree structure.

Finally, calling the exec() method of the QApplication object in the last line of the small application starts the event loop. As mentioned when discussing the 'Hello World' example (see Section 3.1), it will wait for application events (e.g. keyboard or touchscreen events) and will forward them to the appropriate class in our application. Even though we did not set up any event handlers, the quit() method of QApplication is automatically called when the user closes the application through the red *X* in Windows or the red button on a phone, thus exiting it. If we were not to call a.exec(), but instead return 0, the application would terminate immediately without becoming visible on the screen. Of course, the button labelled 'Exit' does not yet have any functionality.

3.2.2   Object Ownership and Memory Management

Especially if your background is in mobile development, you might wonder why the previous example did not delete the allocated objects. The window object is created on the stack using QWidget window. When it goes out of scope at the end of the main() method, the memory allocated for the object is automatically released. However, the other objects are created on the heap and not explicitly deleted by our application. The reason is that Qt takes over some of the memory management.

All of the classes we have been using in the example are ultimately derived from the QObject base class. One of the resulting advantages is that QObject can store object hierarchies. In our case, window is used as the parent object and the four other objects are its children – see Figure 3.3 for the resulting object tree. The QObject base class provides various methods to query or change the object tree manually.

When the parent object is deleted, it automatically deletes its children as well. For this to work, the objects have to lie on the heap – which is why they were created using new. Only the parent object should be created on the stack. In our example, the window object deletes the other objects (layout manager, slider, spinbox and the button) when it goes out of scope at the end of the main() method and is itself destroyed.

While the source code suggests that the user interface widgets are children of the layout manager instance, Qt automatically assigns the widget that owns the layout manager as the parent of the child widgets. This is because a widget can only have another widget as a parent, but no layout. However, it is possible to nest layouts.

3.3 Signals and Slots

After our first steps with the visuals, it is time to take a look behind the scenes to understand how to make the application interactive. The QObject base class, which we have just introduced for handling object hierarchies, defines additional functionality and metaphors. The most important of these is the concept of 'signals and slots' for flexible but safe communication between objects.

Most toolkits use *call-back functions* or *event listeners* for informing other parts of an application about events or status updates. For example, developing an audio player in Symbian OS usually involves deriving a class from an interface. The pointer to this instance is then sent to the external service provider (music player library), which uses call-backs when the file is loaded or when playback has finished. This concept has several disadvantages – the listening class needs to implement a specific interface, the sender has to store and manage pointers to each registered call-back listener and has to check manually if the listener still exists before executing the call-back. Additionally, when storing function pointers, type safety is not checked by C++ for parameters. These drawbacks are addressed by the signals and slots concept of Qt.

3.3.1 Basic Signals

To demonstrate the use of signals and slots, we extend the example from the previous section and add interactivity. The first step equips the 'Exit' button with the expected functionality of closing the application. This is accomplished with the following additional line of code, which should be added after the button has been created:

```
QObject::connect(exitButton, SIGNAL(clicked()),
                 &app, SLOT(quit()));
```

Whenever a specific event occurs – in this case when the button has been clicked – the button object emits a *signal*. Qt widgets have many predefined signals, but you can also add your own signals. The call to QObject::connect() creates a connection between the signal and the slot of another object (see Figure 3.4). A slot is a normal C++ method that matches the signature (parameters) of the signal and that will now be called whenever the signal is emitted. Again, there are many predefined slots in Qt widgets, but you can also add additional slots by sub-classing from Qt classes, including QObject.

The first two arguments of connect() specify the sender of the signal: the emitting class instance and the specific signal that should be bound to a slot. The last two arguments identify the receiving object as well as the slot (method) that should be executed in response to the signal. As the connect() method expects addresses of the objects, the reference operator (&) is not necessary for the exitButton, which is already a pointer.

Flexibility is a big advantage of this scheme. A signal can be connected to multiple slots; each slot can receive signals from multiple source objects. Whenever a signal is emitted, all connected slots are called one after another in arbitrary order (multi-threaded variants are available, see the Qt

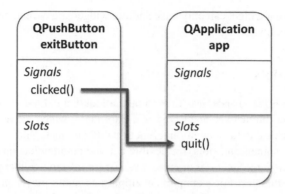

Figure 3.4 Signals are emitted by an object whenever an interesting event occurs. Qt delivers signals to objects interested in these events and calls the connected slots.

documentation). If a signal is emitted, but no matching link to a slot has been established, nothing happens.

The emitter does not know or need to know if anyone in the system is currently waiting for its signals. On the other hand, slots need not be concerned with where the signal originates. These characteristics are vital for information encapsulation and ease development of independent modules that can be dynamically connected at runtime.

In the `connect()` call, both the signal and slot are enclosed by the macros `SIGNAL()` and `SLOT()`. These are necessary because Qt expects string values to be passed to the function. These have to comply with Qt internal standards and dynamically reference the corresponding slots. The macros ensure that these strings are generated correctly based on the specified method names; we do not need to be concerned about this. A visible advantage is that Qt can check when establishing the connection at runtime if the signatures are compatible – thus, it is not possible to connect signals with incompatible slots, which becomes relevant when you want to pass parameters.

3.3.2   Parameters

In many cases, additional information about the event has to be transmitted with the signal. Our example contains a spinbox and a slider widget. What if we want to synchronize those widgets? Changing the value in the spinbox should also update the slider widget and vice versa. Obviously, the receiving widget needs to be informed of the new value whenever the other widget is modified. Only two additional `connect()` statements are necessary to achieve this:

```
QObject::connect(slider, SIGNAL(valueChanged(int)),
                 spinBox, SLOT(setValue(int)));
QObject::connect(spinBox, SIGNAL(valueChanged(int)),
                 slider, SLOT(setValue(int)));
```

Whenever the user changes the value of the slider, this widget emits a `valueChanged(int)` signal. Because of the `connect()` statement, the `setValue(int)` slot of the `spinBox` is then immediately executed. The same thing happens in the reverse direction whenever the value of `slider` is changed. In both cases, the `int` keyword indicates the integer argument that is transmitted to the slot and which specifies the new value.

Of course, this connection in both directions would lead to an infinite 'dialog' between both widgets, where the slider and the spinbox send updated values back and forth. This is prevented by the implementation of `setValue(int)`, which only emits a `valueChanged(int)` signal when the new value is actually different from the previous one.

Note that the argument types are not automatically cast by Qt. For example, if the slot of an own Internet transmission class only offers a slot that accepts values as strings, you cannot directly connect the signal from the slider that transmits an `int` parameter. Neither the compiler nor the linker will notice this; however, a warning will be issued to the terminal window when the `connect()` statement is executed and fails, e.g. when using a different signal of the spinbox:

```
QObject::connect: Incompatible sender/receiver arguments
    QSpinBox::valueChanged(QString) --> QSlider::setValue(int)
```

Therefore, signals and slots are type safe. A failed connection can occur if either the sender or receiver does not exist, or if the signatures of the signal and the slot do not match; `connect()` returns a Boolean value that indicates if the connection was successfully established.

Now that we have seen how to connect two existing classes, the next step is to create your own signals and slots for communicating between different classes in your applications.

3.4   Qt Object Model

Qt extends the functionality of C++ classes to provide more flexibility while still preserving the efficiency of plain C++. The Qt object model mainly offers the following benefits, which we will examine in the sections below in more detail:

- Support with memory management (see Section 3.2.2)

- Signals and slots

- Properties and meta-information.

3.4.1   QObject

The `QObject` class is at the heart of the Qt object model. For a class to take advantage of the additional functionality, it has to be derived from `QObject` and use the `Q_OBJECT` macro in its definition in the header file.

The following example demonstrates a custom class called `SimpleMultiplier` that receives a value through a slot, multiplies it by 2 and emits the result through a signal. Obviously, you would not implement a simple calculation like this with signals and slots in a real-life scenario; however, imagine that the calculation takes a long time or the result needs to be fetched from a web service. In these cases, broadcasting the finished result of the operation through a custom signal is indeed useful.

3.4.2   *Custom Signals and Slots*

Our new `SimpleMultiplier` class is using signals and slots. As described above, it therefore has to be derived from `QObject`. As the class does not display anything on the screen, it is not a widget:

```
1  #ifndef SIMPLEMULTIPLIER_H
2  #define SIMPLEMULTIPLIER_H
3
4  #include <QObject>
5
6  class SimpleMultiplier : public QObject
7  {
8      Q_OBJECT
9
10 public:
11     SimpleMultiplier(QObject* = 0);
12
13 public slots:
14     void startCalculation(const QString value);
15
16 signals:
17     void resultReady(int result);
18 };
19
20 #endif // SIMPLEMULTIPLIER_H
```

The include guards in the first two (`#ifdef ...`) as well as the last line of the header file are common in C++. They are used to avoid problems that could otherwise occur if multiple files in a larger project include the same header file, resulting in a redefinition of a class that is already known to the compiler.

The `Q_OBJECT` macro is inserted right at the beginning of the class declaration. This macro defines several functions that are required for the Qt object model. If you forget to add the macro, this will usually be noticed during the build process:

```
simplemultiplier.h:16: Error: Class declarations lacks Q_OBJECT macro.
mingw32-make[1]: *** [debug/moc_simplemultiplier.cpp] Error 1
```

Through the `SimpleMultiplier` constructor, it is possible to specify a parent object. If defined, this object will get the parent in an object hierarchy through its `QObject` base class. Otherwise, the default value of 0 leads to a zero pointer, resulting in the class not having a parent.

The next block in the class declaration contains the definition of the single custom slot that is offered by `SimpleMultiplier` instances. The accessibility is set to `public` to make them accessible from outside the class – it would also be possible to use the `protected` or `private` access levels, depending on the access requirements.

In contrast to the slots, the `signals:` designator does not need an access control mode. Signals are always public to make communication between different classes useful. Within a single class, it is usually sufficient to use direct function calls. Signals can never have return values, therefore they always use `void`.

3.4.3 Implementing Slots and Emitting Signals

The implementation of the `SimpleMultiplier` class described in the previous section is simple and short:

```
1  #include "simplemultiplier.h"
2
3  SimpleMultiplier::SimpleMultiplier(QObject* parent) :
4          QObject(parent)
5  {}
6
7  void SimpleMultiplier::startCalculation(const QString value)
8  {
9      bool ok;
10     int num = value.toInt(&ok);
11     if (ok) {
12         emit resultReady(num * 2);
13     }
14 }
```

The constructor passes the pointer of the parent object (or 0) to the `QObject` base class.

Notice that the slot `startCalculation(QString)` is implemented as a normal C++ method. Indeed, it is a normal method that you can also call directly from your source code, without the use of signals and slots. However, because of the `public slots:` designator in the header file, it is additionally available as a slot.

In the method implementation, the argument is first converted to an integer through `QString` (see Section 3.5.1). If the conversion is successful, the result of the multiplication by 2 is emitted as a signal.

The argument of the slot is a `const QString`, so that the slot can directly process the output of a standard `QLineEdit` widget. Using call-by-value instead of passing a reference to the string does not generate the overhead you would expect, due to Qt employing implicit sharing – see Section 3.5.1.

In contrast to the slot, the signal is only defined in the header file but not implemented in the `.cpp` file. Qt automatically adds the code to make the signal work through the meta-object compiler.

3.4.4 Meta-object Compiler (moc)

The extended concepts provided by the Qt meta-object model are not defined in C++. Sending Qt-style source code directly to a standard C++ compiler would not work – for example, the `signals:` and `slots:` designators in the header files would not be recognized and result in an error. Two solutions are possible: using a custom C++ compiler, or creating a tool that automatically rewrites the source code.

Qt opted for the second alternative to maintain the flexibility of Qt and to ensure that the Qt code works with every C++ compiler on all supported platforms. Therefore, the source code is extended by the meta-object compiler tool called *moc* before being submitted to a standard compiler. It converts signals and slot constructs to standard C++ by generating additional source code. However, your own source files are never modified – instead, *moc* creates additional files that are included in the build process (moc_myclass.cpp).

If *qmake* is used to create the makefiles (as done by Qt Creator and Carbide.c++), build rules that call *moc* when required are included automatically. This is done for all classes that include the Q_OBJECT macro. In general, the process works without problems. A few limitations are listed in the official Qt documentation (accessible through the help in Qt Creator) under the topic 'Using the Meta-Object Compiler (moc)'. The same article also lists reasons why C++ templates were not suitable for this task.

3.4.5 Connecting Signals and Slots

To demonstrate the use of the SimpleMultiplier class defined in Section 3.4.2, we use a minimal user interface. Similar to the first example from Section 3.2.1, the main() method creates a widget called window which contains two predefined Qt widgets: a text box (QLineEdit) and a label (QLabel) – see Figure 3.5. This time, a horizontal layout manager (QHBoxLayout) is responsible for distributing the available space of the window to the widgets. The include statements are omitted in the following source code; the required header file names correspond to the class names used in the example:

```
 1  int main(int argc, char *argv[])
 2  {
 3      QApplication app(argc, argv);
 4      QWidget window;
 5      QHBoxLayout* layout = new QHBoxLayout(&window);
 6
 7      QLineEdit* input = new QLineEdit();
 8      QIntValidator* validateRange =
 9          new QIntValidator(0, 255, input);
10      input->setValidator(validateRange);
11      layout->addWidget(input);
12
13      QLabel* result = new QLabel();
14      layout->addWidget(result);
15
16      SimpleMultiplier mult;
17
18      QObject::connect(input, SIGNAL(textEdited(QString)),
19                       &mult, SLOT(startCalculation(QString)));
20      QObject::connect(&mult, SIGNAL(resultReady(int)),
21                       result, SLOT(setNum(int)));
22
23      window.show();
24      return app.exec();
25  }
```

After the construction of the QLineEdit object, a validator is assigned to it. Validators can restrict the input of an editor widget. In this case, a predefined integer validator (QIntValidator)

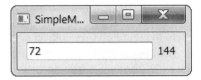

Figure 3.5 A custom class multiplies the input received through a custom slot by 2 and emits the result through a signal.

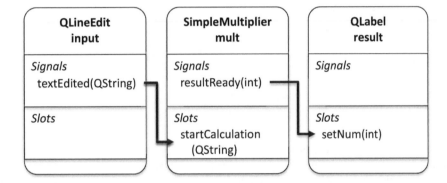

Figure 3.6 The calculation of the custom `SimpleMultiplier` class is triggered by the `startCalculation(QString)` slot. Afterwards, it publishes the results through the `resultReady(int)` signal.

is used, whose first two parameters specify the minimum and maximum value respectively. Own validators can easily be developed; the use of regular expressions is possible as well.

Two signals and slots connections are responsible for responding to the user typing into the text box (see Figure 3.6). The first connects the `textEdited` signal emitted by the `QLineEdit` widget whenever its contents are modified with the `startCalculation(QString)` slot of our own `SimpleMultiplier` class instance. As already described in Section 3.3.2, no automatic type conversion is performed. Because of this, we use a `QString` parameter for the `startCalculation()` slot, as this is the same as the parameter emitted by the `textEdited()` signal.

With the second connection, the result of the calculation is relayed to the label widget. Through these two connections, the result is always updated as soon as the user types in the line edit widget. The beauty of this solution lies in its flexibility. If you wanted to display the result in a second label or transmit it over the Internet, you would simply create another connection that binds the signal to a second slot.

3.4.6   Properties and Meta-information

Properties are another Qt extension to the standard C++ object system. They can be added to classes or class instances and behave like member variables, the main difference being that these can not only be declared in the class header file (through a specific Q_PROPERTY() macro), but even be added dynamically at runtime. This concept is extensively used for the user interface components. The following code discovers and queries the properties of a standard QPushButton instance named but:

```
1  QPushButton but("Hello Property");
2  // Get meta object of target object
3  const QMetaObject *metaobject = but.metaObject();
4  // Number of properties
5  int count = metaobject->propertyCount();
6  for (int i=0; i<count; ++i) {
7      // Retrieve current property
8      QMetaProperty metaproperty = metaobject->property(i);
9      // Print name and value to debug out
10     const char *name = metaproperty.name();
11     QVariant value = but.property(name);
12     qDebug() << "Name:" << name << ", value:" << value;
13 }
```

The result will be 71 defined properties. These range from layout parameters like the position and size, through visibility and button text, up to the locale being used.

Additionally, the QMetaObject instance created for each QObject sub-class provides information about the class name of your object, its super-class or the available meta-methods (signals, slots). While this is usually not required for standard application development, it can be useful for meta-applications like scripting engines.

3.5   User Interface

Qt is often considered as a UI toolkit that allows the creation of a UI that works on multiple platforms. That is only a tiny part of the truth, as Qt is much more than this and provides many other helpful services and modules to application developers. In later sections, we will take a look at some of those, like network or XML support (see Section 3.7). Of course, the UI is still an essential part of almost all Qt applications, so we will start with that.

3.5.1   Handling Text through Implicit Sharing

Almost every application requires text in some form. Therefore, we first take an in-depth look at how to work with text and strings.

UI classes especially are usually derived from QObject as described in the previous sections. However, many other classes do not require signals, slots or automatic memory management. As a result, they are not derived from QObject. A prime example is QString, which stores text on the heap in Unicode format. It can be compared with the new LString class or the RBuf descriptor

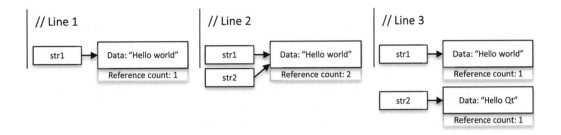

Figure 3.7 For QString objects, data is automatically only copied when needed (implicit sharing).

in Symbian OS. QString comes with plenty of overloads and functions, making it easy to use. For example, during initialization, it automatically converts the const char* data to Unicode in the following scenario:

```
QString str1 = "Hello world";
QString str2 = str1;
str2.replace("world", "Qt");
```

After executing this short segment of code, str1 will still contain its original 'Hello world' text, whereas str2 now reads 'Hello Qt'. This is exactly what you would expect and all that you usually need to care about. Especially when working on mobile devices where memory is limited, it is interesting to know that Qt automatically applies the concept of *implicit sharing*.

While the second line of the code above actually assigns the value of str1 to str2, Qt does not copy it right away (see Figure 3.7). Instead, only the pointer is passed and both variables still reference the same text buffer on the heap (*shallow copy*). To make this mechanism safe, (atomic) reference counting is used for the data. Only when the contents of str2 are modified does Qt have to make both strings separate in memory and perform a *deep copy*. This happens behind the scenes, without intervention from you as a developer. As a result, both the speed and memory usage are optimized.

Additionally, it is therefore usually not necessary to pass pointers to strings for parameters, as call-by-value does not actually copy the contents of the string. The same mechanism is also employed by other classes, e.g. the QImage class for loading and saving images. Using the QSharedDataPointer class, you can easily use implicit sharing for your own classes.

3.5.2 Internationalization

While internationalization might not be important for your first steps with desktop applications, it is usually vital for mobile applications. Users commonly expect localized content on their mobile device.

As a result, native C++ applications for Symbian OS tightly integrate internationalization. For the UI, C++ resource files are used. All strings are externalized to an additional file. Different language variants can then easily be created by including the corresponding file. All localized resource files are shipped with the .sis installation file, whereas usually only the one corresponding to the current phone language is installed. Only if your application does not include the required language will the user get the choice of which other language is preferred. In the application source code, utility classes like `StringLoader` are responsible for loading text from resource files into memory (descriptors).

The process of translating text is different in Qt. The aim is not to kick all text out of the source code, but instead to embed the default language directly into the code (usually English) and if necessary to replace the text through external translation files at runtime. This makes the code easier to write, maintaining at the same time the advantages of having extra translation files. Specific Qt tools help with generating and working with these files. Additionally, the `QObject` base class enables easy integration of translated text even in special cases (e.g., plurals), whereas the resource file approach of Symbian OS mostly requires manual solutions.

Translating Text

For basic translation, all you need to do is to enclose the string in the source code with `tr()`, a method provided by `QObject`. The following example demonstrates the initialization of a label widget with localizable text:

```
QLabel* label = new QLabel(tr("Hello World"));
```

Of course, translation is often not this straightforward. The word order of languages especially has an effect on dynamic text – when inserting for example a file name into a status message, it might have to be placed at a different position for different languages. Additionally, numbers might require different text for singular and plural, depending on their value. If the context is relevant for correct translation, you can provide a textual description of the situation, which will then be visible only to the translator. Take a look at the help section of Qt Creator for instructions on how to handle those situations.

Text written in the source code is the default language. Add any additional translations to the project file, in this case for German and French:

```
TRANSLATIONS = demo_de.ts \
               demo_fr.ts
```

To extract all translatable strings from your source code and to generate the translation files (`.ts` – translation source), call the tool `lupdate <.pro-filename>`. It parses all files registered in the project file under SOURCES, HEADERS and FORMS and generates the `.ts` files, which are based on an XML format. If you add additional text later on, further calls to the same tool will update the existing `.ts` files.

While it is possible to work directly on the `.ts` files, a more convenient way is to use Qt Linguist. This application provides a convenient UI for the translation process, which can easily be used by external translators without technical proficiency. The tool also provides a preview (if Qt Designer was used for generating the UI) and validation features.

After all strings have been translated and are marked as 'finished', run `lrelease <.pro-filename>`. The tool generates compact binary `.qm` files out of the XML-based `.ts` files, which you can ship with your applications or embed into the executable file.

The only remaining task is to load the translation files accordingly. Usually, the `QTranslator` class is initialized at the beginning of the `main()` method:

Locale: de_AT (Austrian dialect of German language)

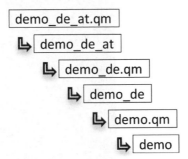

Figure 3.8 If needed, Qt will automatically try to find more generic versions of the translation file.

```
1  // Get locale of the system
2  QString filename = QString("demo_%1").arg(QLocale::system().name());
3  // Load the correct translation file (if available)
4  QTranslator translator;
5  translator.load(filename.toLower(), qApp->applicationDirPath());
6  // Adds the loaded file to list of active translation files
7  app.installTranslator(&translator);
```

The first line retrieves the current system locale, which is returned as a string consisting of a language code and a country code (e.g. *de_AT* for Austrian German). QTranslator first tries to load the specific translation file. If this is not available, it will go through more generic variants step by step to find a suitable translation (see Figure 3.8). For example, if you only provided a generic German translation, the class would automatically load the *de* file if you did not provide specific translations for Austria (*de_AT*) or Switzerland (*de_CH*).

If a suitable file has been found, the work is done and your application is translated. Adding additional languages is just a matter of creating more translation files and adding them to the project file.

3.5.3   Widgets, Dialogs and the Main Window

When developing bigger applications, the approach of simply creating various widgets in the main() method will soon reveal its limits. Of course, Qt offers more flexible and powerful approaches. These include sub-classing widgets, dialogs or using the main window.

Sub-classing Widgets

A common approach for creating a UI is to derive a custom class from the generic QWidget base class. Next, add individual UI widgets like labels, buttons, etc., as member variables and create them in the constructor. That way, UI elements that belong together are encapsulated in a single class, which also happens to be a widget. Modifications or additions do not influence the rest of the

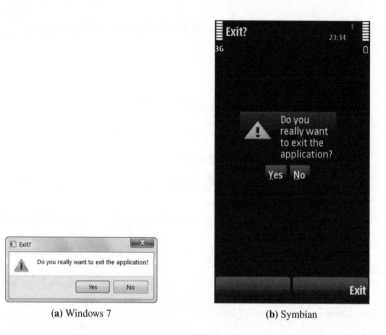

(a) Windows 7   **(b)** Symbian

Figure 3.9 Predefined dialogs for common usage scenarios are provided by Qt – this example shows the warning dialog. (a) Application running on Windows 7. (b) Same application on Symbian.

application. This can be compared with the containers in the traditional Symbian architecture, which are controls themselves, but only serve to manage sub-controls that are the visible UI elements.

Dialogs

In addition to sub-classing widgets, it is also possible to use dialogs. These are intended to be used for in-between information, like asking the user if an Internet connection is to be established (yes/no). If a dialog window is closed, the whole application is usually not terminated.

Similar to widgets, it is common to sub-class `QDialog`, which is itself derived from `QWidget`. Therefore, the basic concept is the same – the `QDialog` class just adds additional methods that are useful for dialogs. Qt already comes with different predefined dialogs, e.g. for entering text or numbers, selecting a colour, a file or a font, and many others.

Using predefined dialogs is easy. The following code demonstrates this using a simple message box, which is fundamental for most applications. The box shows a warning message, asking if the user really wants to exit (see Figure 3.9). Two options are offered, the resulting choice being reflected in the integer return value:

```
int ret = QMessageBox::warning( this, "Exit?",
        "Do you really want to exit the application?",
        QMessageBox::Yes | QMessageBox::No );
```

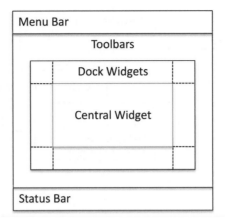

Figure 3.10 The standard layout of a main window on a desktop platform.

By default, this dialog is *modal*. This means that the dialog window is always in front of the parent window. Additionally, the parent is blocked until the dialog returns – interaction is only possible with the dialog as long as it is possible. Of course, you can also create non-modal dialogs. This can be useful, for example, for a search dialog in a text editor application. Such a dialog should stay in the foreground so that the user can search for the next word, but still allow interaction with the editor.

Main Window

Essentially, the QMainWindow represents a predefined layout for the application window, which already defines several components that standard UI applications commonly need. This includes toolbars, dock widgets, a menu and a status bar (see Figure 3.10). The *central widget* represents the main window content (= the workspace for the user).

Of course, creating a layout like that is also possible with dialogs and widgets; however, using the main window is more comfortable and ensures a consistent appearance across multiple platforms. For example, menu commands are automatically mapped to the *Options* menu of the left softkey on Symbian. To create your own main window, derive it from the QMainWindow class. See Section 3.7.3 for an example.

3.6   System

Usually, UI-based applications are event based. They wait for the user to interact in order to start working on the requested task. Compared with continuously polling for status changes ('is the user currently pressing a button?'), sending events to a sleeping application saves a considerable amount of processing time and thus battery life. This section takes a look at how to work with events and timers in Qt.

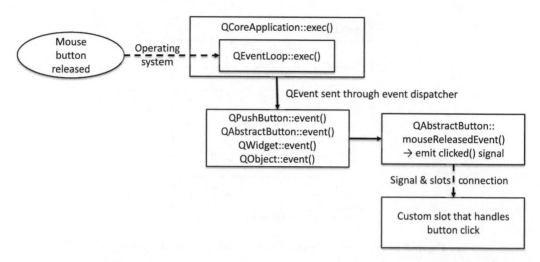

Figure 3.11 This diagram demonstrates in a simplified way how an actual hardware event is translated into a QEvent and then a signal that is handled by your own custom slot.

3.6.1   Events

Events are generated in response to user actions (touch events, keyboard presses, etc.) or by the system (e.g. when a window is shown for the first time). Up to now, we have only been concerned with using predefined widgets. Usually, you will not be in touch with events in this case. Widgets like the QPushButton already include event handlers that emit corresponding signals in response to events, e.g. the clicked() signal when an appropriate mouse or keyboard event is received. Therefore, events are mostly important when **implementing** a widget of your own or if you require to modify the behaviour of an existing Qt widget. Signals on the other hand are important when **using** a widget or for internal communication within your own application.

Figure 3.11 shows a schematic overview of the relation between events and signals and slots through the example of a mouse release event being delivered to a button. First, the hardware event is delivered to the event loop of QCoreApplication::exec(). Through an event dispatcher, the QEvent is then sent to the virtual event() method of the appropriate QObject – in this case, it is a QPushButton. The generic event() method then calls a specific event handling method suitable for this kind of event (mouseReleasedEvent()). This also leads to a clicked() signal that is emitted by the QPushButton. The signal is finally delivered to your own custom slot that starts the appropriate action for the mouse click on the button.

Event Delivery

Events can be generated in two different ways. The first event is concerned with native system window events, like queries to redraw the screen. QCoreApplication::exec(), the main event loop, fetches those events from the event queue. System events are then translated into QEvents and sent to relevant QObjects.

Secondly, a QEvent can also be generated by Qt itself. These events are then processed by the same event loop. The QTimerEvent is an example of a self-generated event, which is triggered after a specific time has passed.

The basic QEvent only stores the event type plus a flag where a receiving QObject can indicate if it accepted this event (otherwise, it might be propagated to its parent). Specific sub-classes like QMouseEvent or QPaintEvent extend the QEvent class to store specific information, like the mouse cursor position or the area to redraw.

The QCoreApplication dispatches events to the event () method of the target QObject, with the QEvent object as parameter. In this method, the class usually examines the event and decides whether to handle or to ignore it – therefore, this method can be referred to as event handler. The implementation of event () in the QWidget class distributes common events to specific handler methods like mouseMoveEvent () or paintEvent (). Therefore, you do not have to write your own event handler function for taking care of common events – you only need to override the corresponding predefined handler method from the QWidget base class. Due to the object hierarchy, events are distributed automatically and you do not have to register explicitly for events in standard usage scenarios. For more control, you can write custom event filters and register for events of other QObjects.

3.6.2   Timers and Painting

Among the most common events are timer events. In contrast to a user-generated mouse button click as in the scenario described earlier, this event is generated by Qt itself. It is mainly used to perform processing at regular intervals. Blinking cursors or other animations are good examples of the use of the timer. Support for timers is built into the QObject base class.

To introduce timers as well as repaint events and the basics of low-level painting, the following example draws a slowly rotating square (see Figure 3.12). Regular call-backs of the timer cause the graphics to redraw. The rotation angle of the quad depends on the current system time.

The main () method simply creates an instance of the custom RotateWidget class and calls show () on it, before using QCoreApplication::exec () to start the event loop. As this is similar to the previous examples, the code is omitted here. However, the full source code is available online.

A timer can be started in multiple ways. This example directly creates an object of type QTimer. Then, it connects its timeout () signal to the update () slot of the widget. This results in regular subsequent calls to paintEvent (), which is in turn called as part of the widget redraw process.

The header file of the RotateWidget class is short and simple. Our class is a widget and thus also indirectly derived from QObject, which is required for event and timer support. To support low-level drawing, it overrides the paintEvent (QPaintEvent*) method from the QWidget base class. The method is an event handler that is called in response to paint events:

```
class RotateWidget : public QWidget
{
public:
    RotateWidget(QWidget* parent = 0);

protected:
```

Figure 3.12 A screenshot of the timer example. The quad rotates with the speed of the clock.

```
7       void paintEvent(QPaintEvent* event);
8 };
```

The constructor of the `RotateWidget` class first creates a new timer. As specified above, this example demonstrates the creation of an instance of the `QTimer` object. The supplied parameter specifies the parent of the timer (`this`). It turns the timer into a child of the widget, so that it will be deleted when the parent `RotateWidget` is deleted:

```
1 RotateWidget::RotateWidget(QWidget* parent)
2         : QWidget(parent)
3 {
4     QTimer* timer = new QTimer(this);
5     connect(timer, SIGNAL(timeout()), this, SLOT(update()));
6     timer->start(50);
7
8     setWindowTitle(tr("Rotating Quad"));
9     resize(360, 360);
10 }
```

The `paintEvent()` method is called in response to paint events, which can occur if `repaint()` or `update()` is invoked on the widget (as in our case) or if the widget was obscured and is now uncovered. Qt automatically takes care of double buffering the output. This means that the changes caused by the individual drawing operations are only copied to the screen when the `paintEvent()` method is finished, thus preventing flickering.

The parameter of type `QPaintEvent` contains event parameters for paint events. Most importantly, it contains the region that needs to be updated. Only redrawing a certain region instead of the whole widget can lead to significant performance improvements, especially on mobile platforms. In our case, it is easier to redraw the whole widget contents. The parameter is therefore unused:

```
1  void RotateWidget::paintEvent(QPaintEvent*)
2  {
3      QPainter painter(this);
4      painter.setRenderHint(QPainter::Antialiasing);
5      QColor quadColor(0, 0, 255);
6      painter.setBrush(quadColor);
7
8      QTime time = QTime::currentTime();
9      painter.translate(width() / 2, height() / 2);
10     painter.rotate((time.second() + (time.msec() / 1000.0)) * 6.0);
11
12     painter.drawRect(QRect(-50, -50, 100, 100));
13 }
```

In the paintEvent() method, we first create a QPainter object. This class is used to perform low-level painting on widgets or other paint devices, like bitmaps or a printer. It offers many convenient methods for drawing simple or more complex shapes, as well as text and pixmaps.

In the next few lines of the source code, we adapt the settings of QPainter. The first activated configuration is to prefer using anti-aliasing, which results in less jagged edges of the rectangle due to the use of transparencies. Next, the brush is configured to use a blue colour. The brush defines the fill colour and pattern of an object, whereas the pen defines the outline style.

The next three source code lines ensure the correct position and rotation of the square. Its rotation is directly related to the current seconds and milliseconds – it would be easy to extend the application to create a full analogue clock (see the Qt documentation for such an example). First, the coordinate system of the painter is translated to the centre of the available size of the widget. Next, a rotate command applies a rotation of the coordinate system depending on the current number of seconds.

In the end, a square with a size of 100×100 is drawn at the coordinates $-50/-50$, in order to centre it around the origin of the translated (and rotated) coordinate system.

When you execute the application, you should see the blue square slowly turning clockwise. Figure 3.12 shows a screenshot of this application running on Symbian.

Alternatively, it would be possible to start a timer using the startTimer() method of the QObject base class instead of using QTimer directly. This method returns an ID, which is used to identify and further control the timer. In contrast to using a dedicated QTimer object, no direct connections to the slot can be made with the startTimer() method. Instead, the timerEvent() method of your class will be called at regular intervals. Also, only QTimer supports single-shot timers, which were not required in this example but are often useful.

3.7 Communication

Especially on a mobile phone, communication is a vital aspect of almost every application. Much like Java ME with the *Generic Connection Framework*, Qt features streamlined interfaces that simplify communicating over various 'devices' like sockets, files or even processes. Not only is it easy to

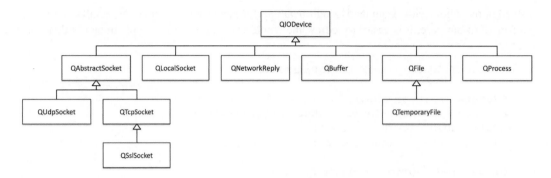

Figure 3.13 Class hierarchy of `QIODevice` and its sub-classes.

replace the employed device using a common base class, but also, when developing distributed or client/server applications, the same code can be used on the Symbian mobile phone as well as on the PC/server side with, for example, a Linux-based operating system.

3.7.1   Input/Output

Figure 3.13 illustrates the classes that inherit from the abstract base class `QIODevice`. These include various socket-related classes, `QBuffer` for reading from and writing to a `QByteArray`, file-related classes for accessing files in the local file system, embedded resources and temporary files, and finally `QProcess` for inter-process communication. Obviously, all these devices behave differently, so `QIODevice` implements the lowest common denominator of all input and output operations.

The most important distinction that still remains is the way of reading data. Sockets and processes are sequential devices; data must be read in one pass. On the other hand, files and `QBuffer` are random access devices, which allow reading at arbitrary positions using `seek()`.

Comparable with Java, Qt provides additional higher level stream classes that simplify reading and writing Qt data types to byte-based streams. `QDataStream` provides serialization of binary data and already includes implementations for C++'s basic data types as well as many Qt data types. By overloading the `<<` and `>>` operators, you can add support for custom data types. For text-based data, the class `QTextStream` helps with reading and writing words, lines and numbers.

These two stream classes take care of lower level necessities like byte ordering and text encoding and therefore help in developing international cross-platform applications.

3.7.2   Files and Streams

To demonstrate the use of files and data streams, we will use a console application without a GUI. In contrast to the previous examples, this type of application only requires `QtCore`. Adding the configuration `console` to the project file (`.pro`) enables console output on Windows. For Mac OS X, the project settings also tell *qmake* not to put the executable inside a bundle:

```
1  TEMPLATE = app
2  QT = core
3  CONFIG += console
4  CONFIG -= app_bundle
5  SOURCES += main.cpp
```

This application does not use a QCoreApplication object, as QFile does not need the event loop – our example is finished after sequentially working through the source code in main(). First, the example creates a file and then serializes three different variables. In the second part, these variables are read back in again:

```
1   #include <QtCore>
2   #include <QDebug>
3   #include <iostream>
4   #include <stdio.h>
5
6   int main(int argc, char* argv[])
7   {
8       // Writing a file
9       QFile outFile("data.dat");
10      if (!outFile.open(QIODevice::WriteOnly)) {
11          std::cerr << "Cannot open file for writing: " <<
12                      outFile.errorString().toStdString() << std::endl;
13          return 1;
14      }
15
16      QDataStream out(&outFile);
17      out.setVersion(QDataStream::Qt_4_5);
18
19      quint32 outValue = 12345678;
20      QTime outTime = QTime::currentTime();
21      QVariant outVar("Some text");
22
23      out << outValue << outTime << outVar;
24      outFile.close();
25
26      // (continued in next listing)
```

At first, our application tries to open the file data.dat for writing. If this operation fails, an error message is printed. This is done using the standard error stream (std::cerr), which is by default directed to the console. The QString returned by outFile.errorString() needs to be converted to a std::string using toStdString(), for which <iostream> has a << overload.

If the file was opened correctly, a QDataStream is constructed using the QFile object (based on QIODevice). In our example, the task of the stream class is to write three different variable types to the file using operator«(), which is overloaded to handle various data types. QDataStream's binary representation of objects has changed in the many years since Qt 1.0 was released, and will continue to do so in the future. In order to maintain forward and

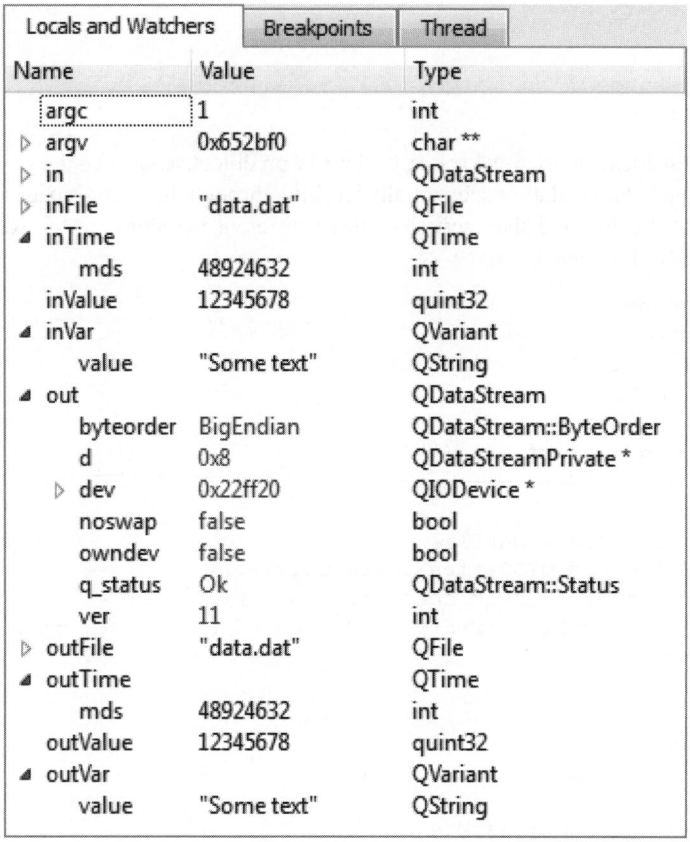

Locals and Watchers	Breakpoints	Thread

Name	Value	Type
argc	1	int
▷ argv	0x652bf0	char **
▷ in		QDataStream
▷ inFile	"data.dat"	QFile
◢ inTime		QTime
mds	48924632	int
inValue	12345678	quint32
◢ inVar		QVariant
value	"Some text"	QString
◢ out		QDataStream
byteorder	BigEndian	QDataStream::ByteOrder
d	0x8	QDataStreamPrivate *
▷ dev	0x22ff20	QIODevice *
noswap	false	bool
owndev	false	bool
q_status	Ok	QDataStream::Status
ver	11	int
▷ outFile	"data.dat"	QFile
◢ outTime		QTime
mds	48924632	int
outValue	12345678	quint32
◢ outVar		QVariant
value	"Some text"	QString

Figure 3.14 Properties of the QDataStream in the debug view of Qt Creator.

backward compatibility, it is helpful to hard-code the version number in the application (e.g. QDataStream::Qt_4_5). This ensures that the data is written and read in exactly the same way.

Additionally, the data format is platform independent. You can transfer data via a network connection from an ARM-based mobile device to an Intel-based PC without problems. In Figure 3.14 you can see that Big Endian data encoding is used by default (see the byte-order property of the out class instance). The data format version of Qt_4_5 equals decimal 11.

Especially for settings files, it is a good idea to extend the example to include a brief file header. This should contain a magic string that allows you to check if the file is really from your application. A version number helps to import correctly old versions of settings files if you decide to expand the file in future versions. See the documentation of QDataStream for an example.

The QVariant data type used for the third variable is a powerful data type. It acts like a union of the most common Qt data types. It stores one type of data and can additionally convert between different types. In our case, the QVariant contains a QString. In addition to serializing the actual content, QVariant additionally saves the type of the variable to the stream, so that it can be read back using a QVariant.

As the outFile object was created on the stack, it will close the file automatically when the variable goes out of scope. However, to be on the safe side and to save resources, it is still a good idea to close resources as soon as you no longer need them.

Reading the file back in works in a similar way to writing the data. After opening the file and creating a QDataStream, we set the stream version to ensure compatibility. Next, the three variables are read back in exactly the same order:

```
1    // Reading a file (continued from previous listing)
2    QFile inFile("data.dat");
3    if (!inFile.open(QIODevice::ReadOnly)) {
4        std::cerr << "Cannot open file for reading: " <<
5                     inFile.errorString().toStdString() << std::endl;
6        return 1;
7    }
8
9    QDataStream in(&inFile);
10   in.setVersion(QDataStream::Qt_4_5);
11
12   quint32 inValue;
13   QTime inTime;
14   QVariant inVar;
15
16   // Read values in same order as they were written
17   in >> inValue >> inTime >> inVar;
18
19   qDebug() << "Variant type:" << inVar.typeName() <<
20               ", contents:" << inVar.toString();
21
22   inFile.close();
23   return 0;
24 }
```

The variable inVar of type QVariant recognized the type that was previously written to the file. The debug output line prints the type of the variable (as text) and then returns the variant as a QString:

```
Variant type: QString , contents: "Some text"
```

Instead of using the standard streams provided by <iostream>, the qDebug() global function (available when including <QDebug>) is used as the output stream. By default, this prints the text to stderr output under Unix/X11 and Mac OS X and to the console (for console apps) or the debugger under Windows. An additional advantage is that Qt data types like QString can be directly serialized, without conversion to a std::string or char*.

You can store data in a very compact way using binary data formats, as demonstrated in this example. Usage is easy through the convenient QDataStream class. As mentioned above, the QTextStream class is specialized on serializing text and can take care of different character encodings. If you prefer a lower level way of handling data, you can use the QIODevice's write() and readAll() functions directly without using higher level stream classes.

3.7.3   Networking and XML

While the QFile class is part of the *QtCore* package that is part of every Qt project, using classes related to communication with the network requires the additional *QtNetwork* extension module. Insert the following declaration into your *qmake* project file:

```
QT += network
```

In the source code, simply include the appropriate header files of the Qt classes in use, as we did before. Alternatively, you can use the directive #include <QtNetwork>, which is a meta-include that contains all the include files for the classes offered by the *QtNetwork* module.

The module provides classes that enable working with both the TCP and UDP protocols, as well as for resolving host names and working with network proxies. Additionally, convenience classes for the higher level protocols HTTP (through the network manager) and FTP are included.

TCP and UDP

The stream-oriented TCP communication protocol is implemented by QTcpSocket. Especially in the mobile context, low-level TCP connections are often preferable to HTTP connections, as they involve less overhead and therefore result in less data to be transferred over often slow wireless connections.

You can use an instance of the QTcpSocket class in your application to handle the network communication. Another option is to derive from the class to customize the behaviour. The operations are performed asynchronously. Status changes and errors are emitted via signals.

As QTcpSocket is indirectly derived from QIODevice, you can use the classes of QDataStream and QTextStream introduced earlier on a socket (see Section 3.7.2). Instead of working with higher level data types, you can directly transmit byte arrays through the read() and write() methods of the socket.

The QTcpServer class makes it possible to accept incoming TCP connections. Depending on the expected number of simultaneously served clients, you can easily implement a server that creates individual threads to serve each incoming client. To compare a simple single-threaded server with the more powerful multi-threaded variant, take a look at the *Fortune Server* example from the Qt SDK.

Due to the nature of the connectionless UDP, no extra server class is required for implementing a UDP server. Instead, the bind() method of the QUdpSocket is used to bind a socket to the specified address and port. Transferring data is done through (usually smaller) datagrams, where each one contains the target address as well as the data. Apart from these differences, the QUdpSocket behaves mostly like its TCP counterpart.

High-Level Network Operations

Qt also provides several high-level classes to perform network operations using common protocols. The QNetworkAccessManager class is responsible for coordinating multiple network requests, which are represented by instances of QNetworkRequest. The request contains information like the request header and the URL. When the request is sent over the network, the QNetworkAccessManager creates a QNetworkReply. The status can then be monitored either through the individual QNetworkReply objects, or through signals of the network manager.

Currently, the network manager allows the use of HTTP, FTP and file access. It supports authentication, encryption, cookies and proxies. QFtp and QFile can be used as dedicated classes for handling the corresponding protocols. The QHttp class has now been superseded by the network request classes mentioned above, which are more powerful.

HTTP is a higher level protocol that is based on TCP. It is a stateless protocol, where requests and responses are always self-contained. The protocol is well known from web browsers, where a request for a website is sent to the server, which then responds with the page contents.

Especially in the mobile world, HTTP-based web services can be even more interesting than downloading whole web pages. The client only requests specific data from the server. The response is usually formatted as an XML file, which can be easily parsed to extract the required information. This concept is also used by the AJAX (Asynchronous JavaScript and XML) requests that made Web 2.0 popular.

XML

Qt provides three ways to parse data formatted in XML. These are encapsulated by the *xml* module, which has to be added to the *qmake* project file in a similar way to the *network* module.

The most flexible approach that allows both reading and writing XML files is the DOM (Document Object Model), a standard of the W3C. When parsing an XML file, the class QDomeDocument builds a hierarchal tree that contains all the nodes of the XML file. This is convenient for applications like web browsers, as they require non-consecutive access to the elements of the XML/XHTML file. The DOM tree can easily be transferred back into an XML file. The obvious disadvantage is the amount of memory required for storing the contents of the whole file – especially on a mobile device.

The Simple API for XML (SAX) is more lightweight. While parsing an XML document, the SAX parser (QXmlSimpleReader) triggers various events, e.g. every time it encounters an opening or closing tag. By overriding the virtual event handler methods, you can merge your own application logic with the parser. SAX resembles a simpler approach compared with the DOM, but makes it more difficult to manipulate the structure of the data, as the data already handled is not stored but discarded instead. Another disadvantage is that parsing source code can easily get confusing, as the logic is distributed over various functions according to the tag type, instead of the currently parsed contents.

The QXmlStreamReader class of Qt improves this aspect. Your application does not have to provide handlers (call-back functions) for the events which are encountered while parsing the XML file. Instead, the application controls the process of parsing the file and navigates by methods that

Figure 3.15 Through parsing the output of the Geocoding web service from Google Maps, the example demonstrates the use of HTTP and XML parsing.

pull tokens from the reader one after another. This is comparable with an iterator with embedded intelligence specifically tailored for XML files.

Especially for tasks that require searching and transforming XML files, the *XQuery/XPath* language is very suitable. It is defined by the W3C[1] to address the need for intelligently querying XML data sources. The main advantage is that it does not require manual procedural programming in C++, but instead directly provides the result of a query formatted in plain text. In Qt, an implementation is provided in the `QtXmlPatterns` module.

Example: Geocoding Web Service

To demonstrate the use of the HTTP and XML APIs as well as the main window, the following example provides a UI for Google's Geocoding web service.[2] See Figure 3.15 for a screenshot of the example application.

Enter the name or address into the upper text box of a location that you want to look up. Clicking the 'Ok' button sends an HTTP request to the Geocoding web service. The response is encoded as an XML file, which contains the longitude and latitude. It is parsed by the `QXmlStreamReader`. Finally, the extracted coordinates of the placemark are converted to numeric values and shown in the second text box.

When searching for the location 'FH Hagenberg, Austria', the Geocoding API will return the resulting XML which is shown below in a truncated version – the full XML file contains some additional details. The Keyhole Markup Language (`kml`) data provides information about the full address of the placemark, the region that it occupies on the map, as well as a point in the centre of this area; this element is called `<coordinates>` and contains the longitude, latitude and altitude (if available, otherwise set to 0):

```
1  <kml>
2    <Response>
3      <name>FH Hagenberg, Austria</name>
4      <Placemark id="p1">
5        <address>
6            Fachhochschule Hagenberg, 4232 Hagenberg im Mühlkreis,
```

---

[1]http://www.w3.org/TR/xquery/.
[2]http://code.google.com/intl/en/apis/maps/documentation/index.html.

```
7        Österreich
8      </address>
9      <ExtendedData>
10       <LatLonBox north="48.3760743" south="48.3612490"
11                  east="14.5310893" west="14.4990745"/>
12      </ExtendedData>
13      <Point>
14        <coordinates>14.5150819,48.3686622,0</coordinates>
15      </Point>
16    </Placemark>
17  </Response>
18 </kml>
```

As mentioned above, using Qt's networking and XML classes requires adding the corresponding modules to the *qmake* project file. When targeting the Symbian platform, you also have to take Platform Security into account. In this concept, access to certain security-relevant parts of the system is only allowed if the corresponding *Capabilities* are specified at compile-time. For example, accessing the network is only allowed if you specify in the project file that your application might require it (the capability is called *NetworkServices*).

Additionally, the certificate that is used to sign the packaged application has to be sufficient for the requested capabilities. By default, the IDEs create a self-signed certificate on your PC when you first build an application. While this certificate is sufficient for using basic capabilities like network access, a security warning will be shown during installation, informing the user what the application might do and that it does not originate from a trusted supplier. For commercial distribution, or if you want to access more restricted areas of the phone (e.g. if you want to simulate key presses for the whole system), the self-signed certificate is no longer 'mighty' enough. See the *Symbian Signed* website[3] for more details on how to use these capabilities for development and on how to obtain a trusted certificate for commercial release.

For our web service example, the standard self-signed certificate is sufficient if we can live with the security warning during installation on a Symbian device. However, do not forget to add the capability to the project file to indicate that your application will want to use the network – if you forget to do so, connection attempts will fail at runtime:

```
1 HEADERS += xmldataview.h
2 SOURCES += xmldataview.cpp \
3     main.cpp
4 QT += network xml
5 symbian:TARGET.CAPABILITY = NetworkServices
```

Setup
As usual, the `main.cpp` file simply creates an instance of the UI class, which is called `XmlDataView` in this example. If the application is executed on a Symbian OS device, it is shown full screen (non-full-screen applications are not common on Symbian). In a desktop environment, the window is shown using the default size. This distinction is executed by a preprocessor directive.

---

[3]http://www.symbiansigned.com/

```
 1 int main(int argc, char* argv[])
 2 {
 3     QApplication app(argc, argv);
 4     XmlDataView geoWindow;
 5 #if defined(Q_OS_SYMBIAN)
 6     geoWindow.showMaximized();
 7 #else
 8     geoWindow.show();
 9 #endif
10     return app.exec();
11 }
```

The class declaration reveals that XmlDataView is derived from QMainWindow, which was described in Section 3.5.3:

```
 1 class XmlDataView : public QMainWindow
 2 {
 3     Q_OBJECT
 4 public:
 5     XmlDataView(QWidget* parent = 0);
 6
 7 public slots:
 8     // Send the HTTP request to retrieve the resulting XML file
 9     void retrieveXml();
10     // Handle the network response, which contains the XML file
11     void handleNetworkData(QNetworkReply *networkReply);
12
13 private:
14     // Private function that parses the XML returned from the web service.
15     void parseXml(const QString &data);
16
17 private:
18     QNetworkAccessManager networkManager;
19
20     // Ui-Elements
21     QLineEdit* locationEdit;
22     QLineEdit* resultEdit;
23
24     // Parsed coordinates from the XML file
25     QString coordinates;
26 };
```

Our class provides two slots, which are executed in response to signals emitted by the UI and the network connection. Two QLineEdit objects are stored as instance variables, as the application needs to interact with the text content. It is not required to keep a pointer to the 'Ok' button, as we will just connect its clicked() signal to the slot that starts the lookup process. All three UI widgets are defined as children of the main window's central widget, so they will be automatically deleted when the main window is deleted due to Qt's object hierarchy (see Section 3.2.2).

Now, let us take a look at the implementation of this class:

```
XmlDataView::XmlDataView(QWidget* parent)
        : QMainWindow(parent)
{
    setWindowTitle(tr("Geocoder"));
    statusBar()->showMessage(tr("Welcome"));

    QWidget* cw = new QWidget();
    QVBoxLayout* lay = new QVBoxLayout(cw);
    locationEdit = new QLineEdit();
    lay->addWidget(locationEdit);
    QPushButton* okButton = new QPushButton(tr("Ok"));
    lay->addWidget(okButton);
    resultEdit = new QLineEdit();
    lay->addWidget(resultEdit);
    setCentralWidget(cw);

    connect(locationEdit, SIGNAL(returnPressed()),
            this, SLOT(retrieveXml()));
    connect(okButton, SIGNAL(clicked()),
            this, SLOT(retrieveXml()));
    connect(&networkManager, SIGNAL(finished(QNetworkReply*)),
            this, SLOT(handleNetworkData(QNetworkReply*)));
}
```

The constructor contains relatively few surprises. First, it configures the UI. The main window's status bar is used to inform the user of the current state. A central widget of the basic type QWidget is used as the parent object, which stores the layout and the three UI elements and is then handed over to the main window through setCentralWidget().

The last part of the constructor deals with the signals and slots connections. The first two connections ensure that both methods create a network request: clicking on the Ok button as well as pressing the Enter key while the locationEdit element has keyboard focus.

Instead of tracking the progress of individual requests we simply connect the finished() signal of the network manager to the handleNetworkData() slot. As the name already implies, the signal will be executed when processing of the network request has finished.

Submitting the HTTP request

Next up in the logical application structure is the slot called retrieveXml():

```
void XmlDataView::retrieveXml()
{
    QString query = locationEdit->text();
    if (query.isEmpty())
        return;
    query.replace(' ', '+');

    QUrl url("http://maps.google.com/maps/geo");
    url.addEncodedQueryItem("q", query.toUtf8());
```

```
10     url.addEncodedQueryItem("output", "xml");
11     url.addEncodedQueryItem("oe", "utf8");
12     url.addEncodedQueryItem("sensor", "false");
13     url.addEncodedQueryItem("key", "abcdefg");
14
15     networkManager.get(QNetworkRequest(url));
16  }
```

This method first retrieves the text from the `locationEdit` widget. Space characters are then transformed into + signs and the final location string is embedded into the full query URL. This is achieved through the `QUrl` class, which provides a convenient interface for working with URLs. The `addEncodedQueryItem()` method is used to add the parameters to the network request. The automatically applied encoding replaces all non-ASCII and control characters with a percentage-encoded format. The maps key (*abcdefg*) is for demo purposes only; you will have to request your own free key from Google. Finally, the request is submitted. The method returns immediately and the request is queued and executed asynchronously in Qt's event loop.

Parsing the XML response

As soon as the network response is available, Qt will call our `handleNetworkData()` slot as a result of the connection that we set up in the constructor:

```
1  void XmlDataView::handleNetworkData(QNetworkReply *networkReply)
2  {
3      if (!networkReply->error())
4          parseXml(networkReply->readAll());
5      else
6          statusBar()->showMessage(tr("Network error: %1").arg(networkReply
               ->errorString()));
7      networkReply->deleteLater();
8  }
```

The private `parseXml()` method (see below) is only executed if the network request completed successfully. Otherwise, we print the error message to the status bar of the main window. After the response has been processed, calling `deleteLater()` schedules the object for deletion. This will happen as soon as the control returns to the event loop:

```
1   void XmlDataView::parseXml(const QString &data)
2   {
3       QXmlStreamReader xml(data);
4       coordinates.clear();
5       while (!xml.atEnd()) {
6           xml.readNext();
7           if (xml.tokenType() == QXmlStreamReader::StartElement)
8           {
9               if (xml.name() == "coordinates")
10              {
11                  coordinates = xml.readElementText();
12                  QStringList l = coordinates.split(',');
13                  if (l.count() == 3) {
```

```
14        statusBar()->showMessage(tr("Successfully received
             XML data"));
15        double longitude = l.at(0).toDouble();
16        double latitude = l.at(1).toDouble();
17        resultEdit->setText("Lat: " + QString::number(
             latitude)
18                         + ", Long: " + QString::number(
                             longitude));
19                     }
20                 }
21             }
22         }
23     if (coordinates.isEmpty())
24     {
25         statusBar()->showMessage(tr("No valid coordinates found in
              network reply"));
26     }
27     if (xml.error()) {
28         qWarning() << "XML ERROR:" << xml.error() << ": " << xml.
              errorString() << " (line " << xml.lineNumber() << ")";
29     }
30 }
```

The QXmlStreamReader class in parseXml() behaves like an iterator. Through the xml.atEnd() call, the while loop checks whether the parser has reached the end of the currently available data. This might also be the case if there was an error while parsing the XML document (e.g. if it is not well formed, meaning that it does not comply with XML syntax rules).

In case the XML reader has not yet reached the end of the available data, readNext() jumps to the next token. We are only interested in the local name of the XML tag start elements. More specifically, we are waiting for the *coordinates* tag. Once this tag is found, readElementText() continues reading the stream up to the corresponding XML tag end element and returns all text in between, which is appended to our coordinates string variable.

If the Geocoding API was happy with the request, the QString coordinates member variable now contains the longitude, latitude and altitude of the placemark. The three values are separated by commas. This character is used to split the string into a QStringList, a list of strings (inherited from QList<QString>). In case the string actually contains the expected three values, we set them as the new text for the resultEdit widget.

This completes the implementation of the Geocoding example, which incorporates many of the concepts introduced in this chapter. You should now have a solid basic knowledge of Qt and be prepared for your first steps in writing your own Qt applications. Of course, Qt provides many more interesting features and modules like data models, SQL, threading and more advanced graphics. These are well worth taking a look at – but, for now, you should dive deeper into the mobile world and learn more about using Qt on your Symbian handset.

Bibliography

Blanchette J and Summerfield M 2006 *C++ GUI Programming with Qt 4*. Prentice Hall PTR, Upper Saddle River, NJ.

Ezust A and Ezust P 2006 *An Introduction to Design Patterns in C++ with Qt 4 (Bruce Perens Open Source)*. Prentice Hall PTR, Upper Saddle River, NJ.

Jakl A 2009 Symbian course materials: `http://www.symbianresources.com/`.

Molkentin D 2007 *The Book of Qt 4: The Art of Building Qt Applications*. No Starch Press, San Francisco.

Qt Development Frameworks 2009 Qt reference documentation: `http://qt.nokia.com/doc/`.

Thelin J 2004 The independent Qt tutorial:
   `http://www.digitalfanatics.org/projects/qt_tutorial/chapter02.html`.

4

Qt Mobility APIs

Tommi Mikkonen, Tony Torp and Frank H.P. Fitzek

This chapter introduces the very first Qt Mobility APIs. The goal of these APIs is to enable the use of mobile phone functionalities in Qt applications. The APIs are easy to use and are designed for cross-platform usage.

4.1 Introduction

In the previous chapters, we introduced the main concepts of general cross-platform Qt. As demonstrated, the Qt framework introduces a powerful way to create cross-platform user interface applications. Moreover, the general cross-platform portion of Qt also provides APIs for implementing the most important system features, including facilities such as example networking, file-related functionality and multi-threading, to name but a few. By their nature, these system features exist on all platforms – including both the portable and desktop environments. Consequently, it is only natural that they are provided for cross-platform development as an integral part of the general Qt.

However, portable devices like smart phones have many special features. These escape the common cross-platform Qt libraries. For example, location information and mobile messaging systems are some features that are typically applicable to portable systems only. Since Qt is now supported by a number of mobile platforms, a new set of APIs for utilizing mobile features in a cross-platform fashion is becoming a practical necessity. The Qt Mobility package implements a set of APIs that grants access to the most commonly needed mobility features without forcing the developer to implement platform-dependent native code like Symbian C++.

The Qt Mobility project v1.0 (`http://qt.gitorious.org/qt-mobility`) delivers a set of new APIs to Qt. These APIs provide access to features that are well known from other mobile programming systems, such as Python or Mobile Java. Furthermore, as in any other mobility library, these APIs allow the developer to use mobility-related features with ease from a single framework and apply them to phones, netbooks and desktop computers, assuming of course that the associated facilities are available in the device in the first place.

The APIs of the Qt Mobility project are real cross-platform APIs. Therefore, the framework not only improves many aspects of a mobile development experience by simplifying the use of associated

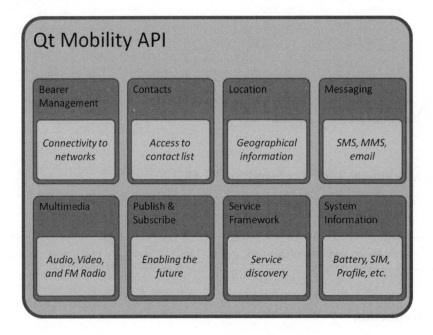

Figure 4.1 Qt Mobility APIs.

technologies, but also has applicability beyond the mobile device arena. Consequently, source code can be reused over the Symbian border (which is covered in this book).

In the following we will briefly explain the different parts of the Qt Mobility API (Figure 4.1).

4.2 Bearer Management

The fundamental goal of bearer management is to reduce developers' concerns when locating the best available connection from a list of possible IP bearers and 3G connections. The user can select the best connection, or the connection can be selected transparently so that WLAN roaming can occur seamlessly.

The bearer management API controls the connectivity state of the system. With the bearer management API, the user can start or stop communication interfaces and roam between access points in a transparent fashion.

Some examples of the bearer management functionality are listed below:

- On-demand use of an appropriate access point. When a user starts to use a browser, the appropriate access point is selected from available ones and a connection is made transparently.

- Always-on applications – such as email or IM – roam automatically between cellular packet data and WLANs. The application developer is in control and if needed the application can gracefully close TCP connections over the old bearer after setting up new TCP connections over the new bearer, for example.

- The application developer can create a settings user interface, where the user can select a certain connection to be used with the application.

- A connection manager application can be implemented with Qt. This application enumerates available connections, shows counters and allows the user to connect or disconnect.

4.2.1   Creating a Network Session

QNetworkConfigurationManager is a class that manages the network configurations provided by the system. Class QNetworkConfiguration provides an abstraction of access point configurations. The following code example illustrates how a network session can be established without any user interaction:

```
1   QNetworkConfigurationManager configurationManager;
2   const bool canStartAccessPoint = (configurationManager.capabilities()
        & QNetworkConfigurationManager::BearerManagement);
3   QNetworkConfiguration configuration = manager.defaultConfiguration();
4   if ( configuration.isValid() || !canStartAccessPoint )
5       return;
6   switch( configuration.type() ) {
7       case QNetworkConfiguration::InternetAccessPoint:
8           // System starts the IAP immediately
9           break;
10      case QNetworkConfiguration::ServiceNetwork:
11          // System determines the best IAP available and starts it
                immediately
12          break;
13      case QNetworkConfiguration::UserChoice:
14          // The access point is resolved by asking the user
15          break;
16  }
17  QNetworkSession* session = new QNetworkSession( configuration );
18  session->open();
```

4.3   Contacts

The fundamental use case for a mobile phone is establishing communications. Most commonly this takes place with an already existing contact. Consequently, one of the special use cases of a mobile device is the management of contacts. Therefore, this is one of the most essential mobility extensions for Qt from the developer's viewpoint.

4.4   The Contacts API

This API defines the structure and retrieval of contact data from local or remote backends. The API offers operations such as create, edit, list, delete and lookup contact information, regardless of whether the data is stored locally or remotely.

4.4.1   Creating a New Contact

A contact can be created by creating an instance of the QContact object, adding contact details and saving it to the contact database via the QContactManager class. This is carried out in the following code snippet:

```
1  QContactManager* contactManager = new QContactManager( this );
2  QContact homer;
3
4  // Create name detail
5  QContactName name;
6  name.setFirst("Homer");
7  name.setLast("Simpson");
8  name.setCustomLabel("Homie");
9  homer.saveDetail(&name);
10
11  // Create phone number detail
12  QContactPhoneNumber number;
13  number.setContexts(QContactDetail::ContextHome);
14  number.setSubTypes(QContactPhoneNumber::SubTypeMobile);
15  number.setNumber("555112233");
16  homer.saveDetail(&number);
17  homer.setPreferredDetail("DialAction", number);
18
19  // Create address detail
20  QContactAddress address;
21  address.setCountry("USA");
22  address.setRegion("Springfield);
23  address.setPostCode("33220");
24  homer.saveDetail(&address);
25
26  // Save the contact to the contacts database
27  contactManager->saveContact(&homer);
28  }
```

4.4.2   Finding a Single Contact Detail

The next code example illustrates how to get the phone number of a specified contact. The IDs of contacts are first fetched as a QList of contact IDs. The example takes the first contact in the contact database and gets the phone number for it:

```
1  QContactManager* contactManager = new QContactManager( this );
2  QList<QContactLocalId> contactIds = contactManager->contacts();
3  QContact firstContact = contactManager->contact( contactIds.first() );
4  QString phoneNumber = firstContact.detail(QContactPhoneNumber::
       DefinitionName).value(QContactPhoneNumber::FieldNumber);
```

4.4.3 Editing a Contact Detail

Contacts can be edited by first fetching the contact, changing or adding the required details and then storing the updated contact in the contacts database. This can be achieved with the following piece of code:

```
1   QContactManager* contactManager = new QContactManager( this );
2   QList<QContactLocalId> contactIds = contactManager->contacts();
3   QContact firstContact = contactManager->contact( contactIds.first() );
4
5   // Change the phone number
6   QList<QContactDetail> numbers = firstContact.details(QContactPhoneNumber
        ::DefinitionName);
7   QContactPhoneNumber phoneNumber = numbers.value(0);
8   phoneNumber.setNumber("555123321");
9
10  // Add an email address
11  QContactEmailAddress email;
12  email.setEmailAddress("homer.simpson@email.org");
13  email.setContexts(QContactDetail::ContextWork);
14  email.setValue("Label", "Homer's work email");
15
16  // Save the details
17  firstContact.saveDetail(&phone);
18  firstContact.saveDetail(&email);
19
20  // Save the updated contact to the database
21  contactManager->saveContact(&firstContact);
```

4.5 Location

One of the promises of mobile computing is context sensitivity. Since location is an increasingly important piece of context for many applications, numerous mobile devices offer access to location information. In the case of Qt, the location API is also an important mobile extension.

The location API encapsulates basic geographical information about the user obtained from satellite or other sources, including latitude and longitude, bearing, speed and altitude. It enables a range of geographical applications such as maps. Information provided includes the following:

- The date and time at which the position was reported.
- The velocity of the device that reported the position.

- The altitude of the reported position (height above sea level).
- The bearing of the device in degrees, relative to true north.

Location data sources are created by creating a sub-class of QGeoPositionInfoSource and providing QGeoPositionInfo objects through the QGeoPositionInfoSource:: positionUpdated() signal. Clients that require location data can connect to the positionUpdated() signal and call startUpdates() or requestUpdate() to trigger the distribution of location data. The main classes of the location API are as follows:

- QGeoAreaMonitor – Enables the detection of proximity changes for a specified set of coordinates.
- QGeoCoordinate – Defines a geographical position on the surface of the Earth.
- QGeoPositionInfo – Contains information gathered on a global position, direction and velocity at a particular point in time.
- QGeoPositionInfoSource – Abstract base class for the distribution of positional updates.
- QGeoSatelliteInfo – Contains basic information about a satellite.
- QGeoSatelliteInfoSource – Abstract base class for the distribution of satellite information updates.

4.5.1   Getting and Following the User's Location

The code example below gets registers for getting notifications on changes in user location. The QGeoPositionInfoSource class is used to get the default positioning source of the device. If the source exists, it can use either satellite data or some other positioning method. The user class must create the source and request updates by calling the startUpdates() method. The positioning info is then eventually passed through the positioningUpdated() signal with a parameter containing latitude, longitude, altitude, etc., as location information. This is realized with the following code:

```
1  // Get the default positioning source. If exists, then request updates.
2  QGeoPositionInfoSource *source = QGeoPositionInfoSource::
       createDefaultSource();
3  if (source) {
4      connect(source, SIGNAL(positionUpdated(QGeoPositionInfo)), this, SLOT
           (handlePositionUpdated(QGeoPositionInfo)));
5      source->startUpdates();
6  }
7
8  // Custom slot for getting the updates
9  void handlePositionUpdated(const QGeoPositionInfo &info)
10     {
11         double latitude = info.coordinate().latitude();
12         double longitude = info.coordinate().longitude();
```

```
13    double altitude = info.coordinate().altitude();
14    };
```

4.6   Messaging

A common interface for handling SMS, MMS and email messages is given by the messaging API. The API provides access to numerous operations associated with messaging. It enables messaging services to search and sort messages, notify changes to messages stored, send messages with or without attachments, retrieve message data and launch the preferred messaging client either to display an existing message, or to compose a message.

4.6.1   Creating and Sending an Email Message

Creating messages is quite straightforward. QMessage represents a message object, which can be of various types, such as an email, MMS or SMS message. The required message fields, body, attachments and other data that can be added depend on the message type. The following code snippet creates a new email message and sends it to a specified email address. This is done by the class QMessageServiceAction, which can also be used for retrieving messages and message data and other appropriate messaging-related actions:

```
1  QMessageServiceAction* serviceAction = new QMessageServiceAction( this );
2
3  // Create a new email message
4  QMessage message;
5  message.setType(QMessage::Email);
6
7  // Add required fields
8  message.setTo(QMessageAddress("myfriend.bestis@emailaddress",
       QMessageAddress::Email));
9  message.setSubject("Pictures from our holidays :)");
10
11 // Set message body
12 message.setBody("Here you go!");
13
14 // Add attachments
15 QStringList attachments;
16 attachments.append("Picture1.jpg");
17 attachments.append("Picture2.jpg");
18 message.appendAttachments(paths);
19
20 // Send the message
21 serviceAction->send(message);
```

4.7   Multimedia

Multimedia has become a standard feature in mobile phones. The Qt Mobility API provides access to a multimedia library, which offers an easy way to play and record audio and video in various formats.

In addition to playing and recording, other features can also be accessed using the API. For instance, FM radio can be used through this API. Moreover, slide shows can be invoked using this API.

4.7.1   Playing an Audio File

The following code snippet plays an MP3 song in a remote website. The API sends signals of the progress of the media file playback. The signal `positionChanged()` is emitted with a parameter specifying the audio playback position in milliseconds from the beginning of the audio file. The method `duration()` returns the total playback time of the object media file:

```
1   QMediaPlayer* mediaPlayer = new QMediaPlayer;
2   connect(mediaPlayer, SIGNAL(positionChanged(qint64)), this, SLOT(
        myPositionChangedHandler(qint64)));
3   mediaPlayer->setMedia(QUrl::fromLocalFile("http://music.com/song.mp3"
        ));
4   mediaPlayer->setVolume(50);
5   mediaPlayer->play();
```

4.7.2   Creating a Playlist of Videos and Playing Them in a Video Widget

The class `QMediaPlaylist` can be used to create playlists for media types. `QVideoWidget` is a special widget for video playback. This example creates a video playlist and uses the media player to play back the videos on a video widget:

```
1   QMediaPlayer* mediaPlayer = new QMediaPlayer( this );
2   QMediaPlaylist* playlist = new QMediaPlaylist(player);
3   playlist->append(QUrl("/MyVideos/video1.mp4"));
4   playlist->append(QUrl("/MyVideos/video2.mp4"));
5   playlist->append(QUrl("/MyVideos/video3.mp4"));
6
7   QVideoWidget* widget = new QVideoWidget( mediaPlayer, parentWindow );
8   widget->show();
9   player->play();
```

4.8   Publish and Subscribe

Publish and subscribe is a widely used messaging paradigm, where communication is decoupled from both producers (publishers) and consumers (subscribers) of data. The communication takes place asynchronously, most commonly using an additional data object.

The publish and subscribe API will enable context-sensitive access to information in future releases. The passed data is organized as a tree, with data being able to 'shadow' other data with the 'same key', a string specifying the leaf or node. The context is an example of a context ontology, a defined set of relationships. As the context changes, the values of the objects change but the relationships remain the same. It is intended to be an enabling technology, the basis of a range of future applications.

4.9   Service Framework

It is common for mobile devices to provide device-specific services. Therefore, one of the most interesting mobile Qt extensions is a platform-independent method to discover services.

Within the scope of Qt Mobility APIs, the service framework API defines a unified way of finding, implementing and accessing services across multiple platforms. In terms of the framework, *service* is an independent component that allows a client to perform a well-defined operation. The services are implemented as plug-ins installed on the device and can look for supporting external services running on a central server. Moreover, because the service framework essentially is an abstraction layer, the application does not need to be concerned with the underlying protocol, where the servers are, the hardware peculiarities with networking and other low-level details.

4.10   System Information

Inside every mobile device, there is a lot of information regarding itself. For example, such information may include details of different pieces of included software, connectivity, hardware characteristics, and so forth. For a software developer, this information is important, since applications may need certain hardware features in order to be useful, or require information on the system in order to customize themselves.

The system information API offers access to discover system-related information and capabilities. They are addressed in the following:

Version contains information for a range of supporting software on the device. For example, information is available from the operating system and firmware to the version of WebKit, Qt and the service framework.

Features lists the supported hardware on the device. Features include subsystems such as the camera, Bluetooth, GPS, FM radio, and so forth.

Network keeps information about the network connection (e.g. MAC address) and type of network such as GSM, CDMA, WCDMA, WiFi, Ethernet and others.

Display information provides access to display information (brightness/colour depth) from the system.

Storage information details the presence of various storage devices such as internal, removable, CD-ROM or even if there no devices.

Device information provides access to device information from the system.

Battery status gives the energy status of the battery at certain levels.

Power state details how the phone is currently powered up and whether it is charged or not.

Profile enables the developer to check on the profile settings of this API for silent, vibrating, normal and others.

SIM indicates the presence of a SIM card, dual SIM card or locked SIM card that can be retrieved.

Input method determines the type of input method such as keys/buttons, keypad, qwerty, single touchscreen, or multi-touch.

Screensaver provides access to the screen saver and blanking.

4.10.1   Accessing Device Information

The following code snippet illustrates how to get information synchronously from QSystem DeviceInfo about the underlying system and then request notifications when the state changes. The example snippet here fetches battery status information and then connects to get updates on battery status. Other similar signals can be connected for the Bluetooth state, current profile and power state of the device:

```
QSystemDeviceInfo* deviceInfo = new QSystemDeviceInfo( this );
QSystemDeviceInfo::BatteryStatus batteryStatus = deviceInfo->
    batteryStatus();
connect(deviceInfo,SIGNAL(batteryStatusChanged(QSystemDeviceInfo::
    BatteryStatus)),
            this,SLOT(handleBatteryStatusChanged(QSystemDeviceInfo::
                BatteryStatus)));

void MyClass::handleBatteryStatusChanged( QSystemDeviceInfo::
    BatteryStatus batteryStatus )
{
    if( batteryStatus == QSystemDeviceInfo::BatteryCritical )
    {
        // Do something
    }
}
```

4.10.2   Accessing System Information

The next code snippet demonstrates the simple usage of QSystemInfo. The example code demonstrates how to check which features are supported by the device:

```
QSystemInfo* systemInfo = new QSystemInfo(this);
// Getting the current language and country code of the device
QString language = systemInfo->currentLanguage();
QString countryCode = systemInfo->currentCountryCode();
```

```
5  // Check if the device has a camera
6  if( systemInfo->hasFeatureSupported( QSystemInfo::CameraFeature )
7  {
8      // Take a picture...
9  }
```

4.11 Summary

The motivation of the Qt Mobility APIs is that they can be used on any system as illustrated in Figure 4.2. Other systems such as Windows Mobile or Maemo might not fully support the individual APIs as given in Table 4.1, but over time the holes will be closed and more APIs will be added.

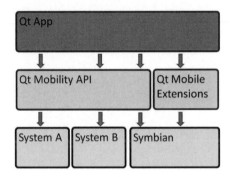

Figure 4.2 Qt Mobility APIs.

Table 4.1 Platform compatibility.

	S60 3rdE FP1 S60 3rdE FP2 S60 5thE	Maemo 5	Maemo 6	Windows Mobile	Linux	MAC
Service framework	Yes	Yes	Yes	Yes	Yes	Yes
Messaging	Yes	No	Yes	Yes	Yes	No
Bearer management	Yes	No	Yes	Yes	Yes	Yes
Publish and subscribe	Yes	No	Yes	Yes	Yes	Yes
Contacts	Yes	No	Yes	Yes	No	No
Location	Yes	No	No	Yes	No	No
Multimedia	No	No	No	No	Yes	No
System information	Yes	No	No	Yes	Yes	Yes

In this chapter, we introduced the Qt Mobility API and the features that can be accessed through it. However, Symbian devices have many other features beyond the cross-platform Qt and Qt

Mobility package. Acceleration sensors and a camera are examples of features that exist in almost all the latest Symbian devices. If you want to utilize those features, you would normally need to implement your application against native interfaces. Forum Nokia Wiki provides a wide set of Qt-like wrappers that hide native Symbian C++ under APIs that provide Qt-like interfaces for utilizing Symbian-specific features. We will cover Symbian-specific mobile extension APIs in the next chapter.

Bibliography

Fitzek HF and Katz M (eds) 2006 *Cooperation in Wireless Networks: Principles and Applications – Real Egoistic Behavior is to Cooperate!* Springer.

5

Qt-Like Mobile Extensions

Tony Torp and Frank H.P. Fitzek

This chapter gives an overview of native Symbian APIs. In contrast to Qt Mobility APIs, these APIs are not that easy to integrate without knowledge of Symbian, but on the other hand new functionalities or flexibility are introduced.

5.1 Utilizing Platform Features beyond Qt APIs

In the previous chapter we introduced Qt Mobility APIs for cross-platform development across various device types. As richly featured smart phones, Symbian devices still have many platform-specific features that Qt libraries or Qt Mobility APIs do not reach. A camera and sensors are examples of those features that exist in every latest Symbian device but are not yet covered by standard Qt APIs. When implementing mobile applications, we are typically willing to take advantage of those features. We basically have two alternative approaches to utilize them from our Qt applications. The first alternative is the native choice. We extend our application with native Symbian C++ using those native Symbian APIs that the platform offers. The drawback with this approach is that then we have to do programming on native Symbian C++, which is known to have a very steep learning curve. The other approach is to make use of prefabricated wrappers offered by Forum Nokia Wiki. They are Qt-like API extensions provided for Qt on Symbian developers for easy utilization of the most important platform features beyond Qt APIs. We can use a Qt-like approach for implementing the functionalities of sensors, a camera, etc., in our applications and we do not need to go too far beyond Qt-like programming.

In the following sections we will introduce the current set of API extensions available for Symbian smart phone development. We call them *Qt-like APIs* because they are not cross-platform Qt APIs (see Figure 1.5) but they are extensions offering Qt-like interfaces for application developers to utilize easily the key features of Symbian devices. Mobile extensions give developers Qt-like access to Symbian smart phone platform-specific features without the need to learn how to program in native Symbian C++. The goal of the APIs is to provide a high enough abstraction level for easy and simple usage for developers.

The extensions introduced in this chapter and given in Table 5.1 do not cover the whole set of extensions offered. Some of them overlap with Qt Mobility APIs and these are excluded from the list.

Table 5.1   List of extensions described in this chapter.

API name	Description
Alarms API	Set an alarm to go on at a particular time
Calendar API	Access appointments in the device's calendar database
Camera API	Take pictures with the device's on-board camera
Installer API	Install a Symbian application from an install package
Landmarks API	List the available landmarks and add new landmarks
Profile API	Read profile information and set the active profile
Sensor API	Detect the acceleration and orientation of the device
Telephony API	Make circuit-switched phone calls, receive call status notifications
Utils API	Launching viewer applications for file types, backlight control
Vibra API	Use the vibra on the device to give physical feedback to the user

Qt libraries, Qt Mobility APIs and the current mobile extensions cover the most important features of Symbian smart phones. If you need to use platform features beyond these and possibly want to implement your own Qt-like Symbian extensions, then you need to utilize native Symbian APIs and learn Symbian C++ concepts. Chapter 6 introduces the main concepts needed for native Symbian development with an example on how to implement Qt-like wrapper APIs.

5.2   How to Use the Mobile Extensions in Your Project

The extensions are API wrappers typically consisting of an object that implements the Symbian C++ API calls and a wrapper class providing Qt-like APIs for your application to use. In order to use an extension you need to add the source files of that extension to your project in your IDE and build them together as part of your application source codes. Using an extension might require certain capabilities to be added to your application project. For example, using the Alarms API typically requires capabilities ReadDeviceData, ReadUserData, WriteDeviceData and WriteUserData depending on the method used. The capabilities are listed in the extension documentation together with the API descriptions. In the next chapter we give an overview of Symbian C++ with an example on how these wrappers are really implemented.

5.3   Alarms

The *Alarms API* can be used for setting alarms, viewing current alarms and removing alarms on the device. The API allows you to set an alarm that goes on or off at a particular time of the day. A list of alarms set on the device can also be retrieved with the API. The main API is class XQAlarms, which can be used to set, modify and remove alarms. Class XQAlarm is used to store alarm data such as category, expire time and message attached to the alarm.

Using the API requires capabilities ReadDeviceData, ReadUserData, WriteDeviceData and WriteUserData.

5.3.1   Getting a List of All Alarms

The following snippet creates a list of alarm IDs of all alarms that have been set.

```
1  // Create an XQAlarms instance and fetch ids
2  XQAlarms* alarms = new XQAlarms(this);
3  QList<int> ids = alarms->alarmIds();
```

5.3.2   Creating a Workday Wakeup Alarm

Alarms can be created by creating an XQAlarm object and then adding the alarm with the XQAlarms instance. The following code example creates a weekly repeated alarm for a weekly report from the current day onwards:

```
1  // Creating a workday wakeup alarm
2  XQAlarms* alarms = new XQAlarms(this);
3  QDateTime alarmDateTime = alarmDateTime.currentDateTime();
4  alarmDateTime.setTime(QTime(15, 0));
5  // Create XQAlarm data object
6  XQAlarm weeklyReport;
7  weeklyReport.setExpiryTime(alarmDateTime);
8  weeklyReport.setMessage("Do weekly report");
9  weeklyReport.setRepeatDefinition(XQAlarm::RepeatWeekly);
10 alarms->addAlarm(weeklyReport);
```

5.3.3   Changing the Time of a Specific Alarm

Existing alarms can be modified. This code example shows how to change the time of a first alarm on the alarms ID list:

```
1
2
3  XQAlarms* alarms = new XQAlarms( this );
4  QList<int> ids = alarms->alarmIds();
5
6  // Create XQAlarm data object to get the data of the existing alarm.
7  XQAlarm alarmToChange = alarms->alarm(ids.value(0));
8
9  QString alarmMessage = alarmToChange.message();
10 int alarmDay;
11 QDateTime dateTime = alarmToChange.expiryTime();
12 if (alarmToChange.repeatDefinition() == XQAlarm::RepeatOnce ||
13               alarmToChange.repeatDefinition() == XQAlarm::RepeatWeekly
                    )
14 {
15
16     alarmDay = dateTime.date().dayOfWeek();
```

```
17  }
18
19  int oldAlarmDefinition = alarmToChange.repeatDefinition();
20
21  // Delete the old alarm
22  alarms->deleteAlarm(ids[0]);
23
24  QDateTime alarmDateTime = alarmDateTime.currentDateTime();
25
26  // Set new alarm time to 15.00
27  QTime newTime = QTime(15, 00);
28  alarmDateTime.setTime(newTime);
29
30  // If the time has passed, we add one day to the alarm time
31  if (alarmDateTime.time() < QDateTime::currentDateTime().time())
32  {
33      alarmDateTime = alarmDateTime.addDays(1);
34  }
35
36  // Create a new alarm based on the alarm data
37  XQAlarm updatedAlarm;
38  updatedAlarm.setExpiryTime(alarmDateTime);
39  updatedAlarm.setMessage(alarmMessage);
40  updatedAlarm.setRepeatDefinition(
41          static_cast<XQAlarm::RepeatDefinition>(oldAlarmDefinition));
42
43  alarms->addAlarm(updatedAlarm);
```

5.3.4 Deleting an Alarm

Alarms can be deleted by the alarm ID. The following code snippet deletes the first alarm from the alarm ID list:

```
1  XQAlarms* alarms = new XQAlarms( this );
2  // Get the list of all alarm ids and delete the first one (index 0)
3  QList<int> ids = alarms->alrmIds();
4  alarms->deleteAlarm(ids[0]);
```

5.4 Calendar

The *Calendar API* provides access to items in the calendar database of the device. Appointments, 'ToDo' notes, anniversaries and other time-specific events are stored in the calendar database. The Calendar API can be used for application access to the calendar database for retrieving, changing and adding items. The main class of the API is XQCalendar, which represents the calendar database. The other classes are as follows:

- XQCalendar – the calendar database

- XQCalendarEntry – an entry in the database
- XQCalendarCategory – an entry category
- XQCalendarAttendee – name, role, etc., of appointment attendee
- XQCalendarAlarm – alarm for a calendar entry
- XQCalendarRepeatRule – for repeating calendar entries
- XQCalendarWidget – widget for showing a month at a time.

Using the API requires capabilities ReadDeviceData, ReadUserData, WriteDeviceData and WriteUserData.

5.4.1 Creating a New Calendar Item

Adding new items to a calendar is fairly straightforward. The XQCalendarEntry instance is created with specified data and then added to the calendar database by using XQCalendar. The following code snippet creates a 'ToDo' note with an alarm attached:

```
1  // Create a calendar object
2  XQCalendar* calendar = new XQCalendar( this );
3  // Create a new ToDo entry
4  XQCalendarEntry entry(XQCalendarEntry::TypeTodo);
5  entry.setStartAndEndTime( QDateTime(...), QDateTime(...));
6  entry.setSummary( QString("Find and buy a new tie") );
7  // Setting an alarm 60 mins prior to the entry
8  XQCalendarAlarm alarm;
9  alarm.setTimeOffset( 60 );
10 entry.setAlarm( alarm );
11 // Add the entry to the calendar database
12 calendar->addEntry(entry);
```

5.4.2 Deleting Calendar Entries

Deleting a calendar entry requires an entry ID for the entry. The entry IDs can be fetched as a list by method entryIds() which returns the complete list of entry IDs. Single calendar entries can then be fetched and data can be checked. The following code snippet deletes all calendar entries after a specified date:

```
1  // Create a calendar object
2  XQCalendar* calendar = new XQCalendar( this );
3  QDate dayOfDoom( 2009, 12, 7 );
4
5  // Get the list of all entry IDs in calendar database
6  // and delete entries after the specified date
7  QList<ulong> entryIds = calendar->entryIds();
8  for (int i = 0; i < entryIds.count(); i++)
9  {
```

```
10     XQCalendarEntry entry = calendar->fetchById(entryIds[i]);
11     if (entry.startTime().date() > dayOfDoom )
12     {
13         calendar->deleteEntry( entryIds[i] );
14     }
15 }
```

5.5   Camera

Most Symbian smart phones come with a built-in camera. The *Camera API* can be used for taking photos. With the API you can first see a preview of the image you might take, then focus the camera and then actually take the photo. The main API class is XQCamera, which provides slots for focusing and capturing a picture. The desired picture size can also be reset from the default of 640×480 pixels. Signals are emitted when the camera is ready, the camera focusing is ready or image capture is completed. The other class of the API, XQViewFinderWidget, is a widget that can be used for previewing an image.

Taking a picture with the Camera API involves a number of steps: first the camera class is initialized, then the viewfinder is started, then the user clicks the capture button to take the photo, then the image is available and can be saved. The following code snippets demonstrate the usage.

Capturing images typically consumes a lot of memory, so this should be considered when several images are open at any one time.

The API indicates an error on possible error situations during opening, focusing or capturing. If the operation fails, the corresponding method returns false and the error code can be fetched by XQCamera::error(). Similarly, starting a viewfinder widget might end up in an error, which can then fetched by XQViewFinderWidget::error().

Using the API requires capabilities MultimediaDD and UserEnvironment.

5.5.1   Camera Initialization

The next code snippet initializes the camera and connects the camera signals to slots in our application. The user class is MyXQCameraUser. The default image capturing size is 640×480 pixels which can be changed by using the setCaptureSize() method:

```
1  class MyXQCameraUser : public QObject
2  {
3      Q_OBJECT
4
5  protected slots:
6      void imageCaptured(QByteArray imageData);
7
8  private:
9      XQCamera* camera;
10     XQViewFinderWidget* viewFinder;
11 };
12
```

```
13
14    // Create a camera object and set the capture size
15    camera = new XQCamera(this);
16    camera->setCaptureSize(QSize(1280,960));
17
18    // Create a capture button and connect it to the camera's capture
          slot
19    QPushButton* captureButton = new QPushButton("CaptureImage");
20    connect(captureButton, SIGNAL(clicked()), camera, SLOT(capture));
21
22    // Connect to the captureCompleted signal
23    connect(camera, SIGNAL(captureCompleted(QByteArray)), this, SLOT(
          imageCaptured(QByteArray)));
```

5.5.2   Using the Viewfinder Widget

The viewfinder is started when the camera is ready. We connect the cameraReady() signal straight to the start() slot of the viewfinder:

```
1  // Initialize the viewfinder, set the source camera and the size of the
        image
2  viewFinder = new XQViewFinderWidget;
3  viewFinder->setCamera(*camera);
4  viewFinder->setViewfinderSize(QSize(256, 192));
5
6  // Start the viewfinder when the camera signals it is ready
7  connect(camera, SIGNAL(cameraReady()), viewFinder, SLOT(start()));
```

5.5.3   Taking a Photo

Clicking the 'CaptureImage' button initializes the image capture process. The button's clicked() signal is connected to the camera's capture() slot. The camera class will emit a captureCompleted() signal when the image capture is completed. You can connect this to a slot in your application that will handle the captured image. The following code stops the viewfinder and the captured image is shown for 5 seconds in the viewfinder widget. Then the viewfinder is started again:

```
1  void MyXQCameraUser::imageCaptured(QByteArray imageData)
2  {
3      // Stop the viewfinder and show the captured image in the viewfinder
4      viewFinder->stop();
5
6      // Get the image data into an image class
7      QImage capturedImage = QImage::fromData(imageData);
8      viewFinder->setImage(capturedImage);
9      camera->releaseImageBuffer();
```

```
10
11      // Restart the viewfinder after 10 seconds
12      QTimer::singleShot(10000, viewFinder, SLOT(start()));
13  }
```

5.6   Installer

The *Installer API* can be used to install and uninstall applications without notifying the user through the standard installation dialogs. So you can use this API silently to install applications or you can create for example your own installation user interface. The Installer API can also be used to get a list of all the applications that are installed on the device. Each Symbian application is identified by the system through a unique application identifier, UID3. The Installer API provides a method for fetching the list of UIDs or names of all applications currently in the system. Installing new applications is done by specifying the full path of the SIS file of the application.

Using the API requires capability TrustedUI from the application.

5.6.1   Installing an Application in the Background without Notifying the User

The following code snippet shows how to install an application from an installation file. On the Symbian platform, the installation package is referred to as a SIS file and has a .sisx extension. After installation is completed, either an applicationInstalled() or error() signal is emitted depending on whether the installation was successful or not:

```
1   XQInstaller* installer = new XQInstaller(this);
2
3   // Connect the signals and slots
4   connect(installer, SIGNAL(applicationInstalled()), this, SLOT(
            installationSucceeded()));
5   connect(installer, SIGNAL(error()), this, SLOT(installationFailed()));
6
7   // Install an example package from the installs folder
8   bool result = installer->install("c:\\Data\\exampleapplication.sisx");
9
10  // Check that the installation started
11  if (!result)
12  {
13      // Installation start failed
14      XQInstaller::Error error = installer->error();
15      // Add possible error handling code here
16  }
```

5.6.2   Uninstalling an Application in the Background without Notifying the User

The snippet below shows how to uninstall an application without informing the user. Each application has a unique identifier, so this is how you specify which application to uninstall. After the process is completed, either an `applicationRemoved()` or `error()` signal is emitted depending on whether the uninstalling was successful or not:

```
XQInstaller* installer = new XQInstaller(this);

// Connect to the applicationRemoved() signal
connect(installer, SIGNAL(applicationRemoved()), this, SLOT(
    uninstallationSucceeded()));
connect(installer, SIGNAL(error()), this, SLOT( uninstallationFailed()
    ));

// UID3 of the application
uint appId = 0x12345678;

// Uninstall the application with the given ID
bool result = installer->remove(appId);

// Check that the uninstall started
if (!result)
{
    // Uninstall failed
    XQInstaller::Error error = installer->error();
    // Add possible error handling code here
}
```

Possible error situations can arise from the system, e.g. not enough memory, security failure, package not supported or installer busy.

5.6.3   Getting a List of all Installed Applications in the Device

The Installer API can be used to get a list of the applications that are currently installed on the device. The list can be fetched as application names or application UIDs:

```
XQInstaller* installer = new XQInstaller(this);

// Get a list of applications by UID
QList<uint> uids = installer->applications().values();

// Get a list of applications by name
QList<QString> applications = installer->applications().keys();
```

5.7   Landmarks

A landmark is a location tag with a name and possible other data such as description, icon, address details. Landmarks are organized in landmark databases, which might be maintained locally on your device or, for example, on a remote server that your device can access over the Internet. The *Landmarks API* provides methods for adding landmarks and listing available landmarks.

The main API class is XQLandmarkManager, which gives you access to the landmark database. It provides methods for adding landmarks and getting the list of currently available landmarks. The class XQLandmark describes a landmark, which can consist of a name, position information, a description and other possible details. Adding a new landmark can typically be related to the current location information, which can be obtained through the Qt Location Mobility API.

Applications using the API require capabilities ReadUserData and WriteUserData.

5.7.1   Creating a Landmark for the Current Location

The Landmarks API enables you to store details about a particular location and the Location API can used to supply the coordinates of your current location. A common use case will be to get current location, query a description from the user and add the newly created landmark to the database. The following code snippet creates a new landmark object with a name and coordinates and adds it to the landmarks database:

```
1   // Create a new landmark and set the name and location information
2   XQLandmark landmark;
3   landmark.setName("Wonderland");
4   landmark.addCategory("Amusement");
5   landmark.setPosition(40.123, 20.321);
6
7   // Add the landmark to the landmark database
8   XQLandmarksManager* landmarksManager = new XQLandmarksManager(this);
9   landmarksManager->addLandmark(landmark);
```

5.7.2   Getting a List of All Landmarks in the Landmark Database

The next code snippet shows how to use the Landmarks API to get a list of all landmarks in the landmarks database. The landmarks can be fetched in one list containing landmark IDs. A single XQLandmark can then be accessed by the ID:

```
1   XQLandmarksManager* landmarksManager = new XQLandmarksManager(this);
2
3   // Get list of all landmark IDs from the database
4   QList<int> ids = landmarksManager->landmarkIds();
5
6   // Go through all the landmark items in the list
7   for (int i = 0; i < ids.count(); ++i)
8   {
9       XQLandmark landmark = landmarksManager->landmark(ids.value(i));
10      qreal latitude = landmark.latitude();
11      qreal longitude landmark.longitude();
12          QString name = landmark.name();
13          QString description = landmark.description();
14          //...
15  }
```

5.8 Profile

A profile defines the sound scheme of when various events like incoming messages or phone calls are received. When the silent profile is active, the phone will not play any sounds when such an event occurs. When the meeting profile is active, a small beep will play in the case of an incoming call or message. The General profile is the usual profile with user-selected ringing tones and message alert tones.

The *Profile API* can be used for changing between different profiles and also for fetching the current active profile. The main class of the API is XQProfile. The method isFlightMode() can be used to check if the phone is in an offline state and the network connectivity is disabled. The profiles API only works for the predefined profiles so custom profiles are not supported. The API contains methods for modifying predefined profiles. For example, ringing tone, message alert tone or ringing volume can be set by simple API calls. The API does not provide methods for creating new profiles or modifying profiles that are not predefined.

Using the API requires capability WriteDeviceData.

5.8.1 Getting the Current Active Profile

The following code snippet shows how to use the Profile API to get the profile that is currently active on the device:

```
1 XQProfile* profile = new XQProfile(this);
2
3 // Get the current profile
4 XQProfile::Profile activeProfile = profile->activeProfile();
```

The active profile is enumerated as:

```
1    enum Profile {
2          ProfileGeneralId,
3          ProfileSilentId,
4          ProfileMeetingId,
5          ProfileOutdoorId,
6          ProfilePagerId,
7          ProfileOffLineId,
8          ProfileDriveId
9    }
```

5.8.2 Setting the Current Profile to Silent

The following code snippet shows how to use the Profile API to set the current profile to flight mode; the network connectivity is then set off:

```
1 XQProfile* profile = new XQProfile(this);
2
3 // Set the profile to Silent
4 bool result = profile->setActiveProfile(XQProfile::OffLineId);
```

5.8.3   Setting the Ringing Volume of the General Profile to Maximum

The following example modifies the general profile by setting the ringing volume to maximum; the vibrating alert to the general profile is also set to 'no vibra':

```
1  XQProfile* profile = new XQProfile(this);
2
3  // Set ringing profile to maximum, i.e. volume level 10
4  bool volume = profile->setRingingVolume(XQProfile::RingingVolumeLevel10,
       XQProfile::ProfileGeneralId);
5  bool vibra = profile->setVibratingAlert(false, XQProfile::
       ProfileGeneralId);
```

5.9   Sensors

There are two types of sensors available through the *Sensor API* extension, namely orientation (Figure 5.1) and acceleration sensors. Orientation sensors can be used for getting the display orientation or, more accurately, the rotation angle of the device. Rotation is defined by the X, Y and Z dimensions, each varying between 0 and 359 degrees (Figure 5.2). The display orientation describes the current orientation in a rough way, specifying the direction in which the device's display is heading. The API for accessing the orientation sensor is XQDeviceOrientation.

You can use the acceleration sensor extension to determine the acceleration of the device. This is useful for detecting movement gestures, such as moving the device up or down. The orientation of the device affects the acceleration sensors due to the acceleration caused by the Earth's gravity. Therefore you cannot assume that the axis values are zero when the device is still. In fact, if the device is in free fall then the value of each axis is zero.

5.9.1   Receiving Notification of Changes in Rotation and Orientation

The following code snippet uses the orientation sensor to receive notification of when the device is rotated in the X direction by at least 15 degrees and when the device orientation changes. The API notifies the client by sending signals orientationChanged() and xRotationChanged(). The latter applies to all coordinates X, Y and Z. The new rotation angle is sent as a signal parameter:

```
1  XQDeviceOrientation* orientation = new XQDeviceOrientation(this);
2
3  // Opens orientation sensor data flow
4  orientation->open();
5
6  // Set the number of degrees the device must rotate
7  // before you are notified. The resolution is set here to 15 degrees
8  orientation->setResolution(15);
9
10 // Start listening X-rotation updates with the resolution set
11 connect(orientation, SIGNAL(xRotationChanged(int)),
12     this, SLOT(rotationUpdated(int)));
```

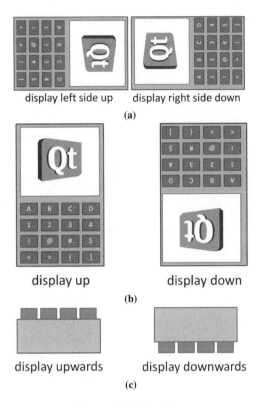

display left side up   display right side down

(a)

display up   display down

(b)

display upwards   display downwards

(c)

Figure 5.1 Orientation.

```
13
14 // Start listening changes in display orientation
15 connect(orientation, SIGNAL(orientationChanged(XQDeviceOrientation::
       DisplayOrientation)),
16     this, SLOT(orientationUpdated(XQDeviceOrientation::DisplayOrientation
           )));
```

The current rotation angle can also be fetched synchronously using the following simple query API:

```
1 // We read the current rotation (synchronous)
2 int xRotation = orientation->xRotation();
3 int yRotation = orientation->yRotation();
4 int zRotation = orientation->zRotation();
```

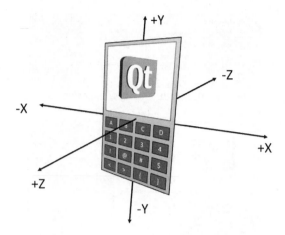

Figure 5.2 The device's own coordinate system.

5.10 Telephony

The *Telephony API* extension brings voice telephony dialling and line monitoring functionality to our applications. The main API class XQTelephony provides methods for making circuit-switched telephone calls and monitoring the call line status (idle, ringing, dialling, connected, hold, etc.). This API can only be used for traditional circuit-switched telephony calls. No packet-switched telephony is supported.

You can also use the Telephony API to inform you when the call line status changes, e.g. when a phone call starts or ends. You can do this by creating an XQTelephony instance and connecting the lineStatusChanged() signal to a slot method in your application.

5.10.1 Making a Circuit-Switched Telephone Call

This simple API opens a voice telephony call to a telephone number specified by parameter:

```
1  XQTelephony* telephony = new XQTelephony(this);
2  telephony->call("+358301234567");
```

5.10.2 Receiving Notification of When Phone Call Status Changes

The call line status can be monitored by using a signal and slot mechanism. The following code shows the connection of the lineStatusChanged() signal to the application's handleStatusChange() slot:

```
1
2  XQTelephony* telephony = new XQTelephony(this);
3  connect(telephony, SIGNAL(lineStatusChanged(XQTelephony::LineStatus,
       QString)),
```

```
4        this, SLOT(handleStatusChange(XQTelephony::LineStatus, QString)));
5
6  // Our slot for handling telephone line status changes
7  void MyTelephoneLineListener::handleLineStatusChange(XQTelephony::
       LineStatus status, QString number)
8  {
9      switch(status)
10     {
11         case XQTelephony::StatusRinging:
12         {
13             // Incoming call. Take action
14         }
15     }
16 }
```

5.11   Utils

The *Utils API* provides assorted platform-specific utilities. The API XQUtils can be used to launch a default viewer application for certain file types. The Utils API also offers a method for applications to reset the system inactivity timer to keep the backlights on. Symbian devices have a background process running and detect user activity on the device. The timer is reset whenever there is some user activity, e.g. key or pen presses or slider movements. If there is no activity for a few seconds the timer expires and the backlight is switched off. The API also provides methods for fetching the file paths of certain stored items such as images, videos or pictures:

```
1  static QString videosPath()
2  static QString imagesPath()
3  static QString picturesPath()
```

The Utils API also has another class, XQConversions, which is very useful when mixing Symbian C++ and Qt code. It provides methods for converting Symbian descriptors and QString and vice versa. The next chapter covers the most important Symbian coding concepts.

5.11.1   *Keeping the Device Backlight Turned On*

The following code has a timer that goes off once every second and uses the method XQUtils::resetInactivityTimer() to reset the system inactivity timer. So this code keeps the background lights of the device on. This API could be useful, e.g. in game applications where the user has to see the board for a while when thinking about the next move:

```
1  XQUtils* utils = new XQUtils(this);
2
3  // Create a timer that goes off once every second and start it
4  QTimer* timer = new QTimer(this);
5  timer->setInterval(1000);
6  timer->start();
7
```

```
8  // Connect the timer's timeout() signal to XQUtils::resetInactivityTime()
9  connect(timer, SIGNAL(timeout()), utils, SLOT(resetInactivityTime()));
```

5.11.2 Launching a File with the Default Viewer Application

The code snippet below launches a system default viewer application for JPEG files:

```
1  XQUtils* utils = new XQUtils(this);
2  utils->launchFile("MyPicture.jpg");
```

5.11.3 Converting between QString and HBufC*

The following simple code snippet allows conversion from QString to HBufC and back again:

```
1  // Allocate the QString
2  QString bookNameString("Qt for Symbian");
3  // Convert to a descriptor
4  HBufC* bookNameDescriptor = XQConversions::qStringToS60Desc(
       bookNameString );
5  // Convert the descriptor back into another QString
6  QString anotherBookName = XQConversions::s60DescToQString( *
       bookNameDescriptor );
```

5.12 Vibra

The *Vibra API* can be used to vibrate the device. The main class of the API is XQVibra, which can also be used for getting the vibration settings from the current profile. Vibration can be started and stopped by invoking methods start() and stop(). The vibration intensity can be set by the method setIntensity(). The intensity value can be between -100 and 100. Intensity value 0 stops the vibration. The actual intensity depends on the hardware.

It is possible that the user has set the vibration off, e.g. in silent mode, so that can easily be checked by the API. The API has an access method currentStatus() which returns the status. The signal statusChanged() is also emitted when the vibration status changes between vibration not allowed, vibration off and vibration on. The status can be fetched by invoking the currentStatus() method.

5.12.1 Switching on the Vibration Function

The code here uses the Vibra API to switch on the vibration function for 2 seconds at 80% intensity:

```
1  XQVibra* vibra = new XQVibra(this);
2
3  // Set the vibration intensity to 50$\%$. Possible values are between
       -100$\%$ and 100$\%$.
4  vibra->setIntensity(80);
```

```
5
6  // Activate the vibra function for 3 seconds
7  vibra->start(2000);
8
9  //...
10
11 // Vibra can be stopped explicitly before the timer by calling
12 vibra->stop();
```

6

Qt Apps and Native Symbian Extensions

Angelo Perkusich, Kyller Costa Gorgônio and Hyggo Oliveira de Almeida

Symbian OS is an open, mobile operating system that is embedded in a large diversity of smart phones today. Symbian OS offers a fully featured framework for developing applications in the C++ language, including modules for networking, concurrency and accessing native smart-phone features. With the increasing power and dissemination of smart phones, the demand for software is also growing. This requires higher level tools to speed up the development and increase software quality. In this context, Qt is the most promising solution for achieving massive and high-quality application development. Developers can use the Qt framework to create new applications and port existing Qt applications to devices running Symbian OS with 5th Edition v1.0, as well as 3rd Edition FP1 and later devices. In this chapter we present an overview of the Symbian OS main features as well as Qt Native Symbian Extensions.

6.1 Data Types and Symbian OS Class Naming Conventions

Instead of using native C++ types, Symbian OS has its own fundamental types defined as a set of `typedefs` in the Symbian header file `e32def.h`. This is necessary to keep compiler independence. Symbian OS types should always be used instead of the native ones. Developers should use `void` when a function or method has no return type, instead of `TAny`.

By convention, there are several class types on Symbian OS, with different characteristics, such as where objects may be created (on the heap, on the stack, or on either) and how those objects should later be cleaned up. When Symbian C++ was created, a native exception handling mechanism, named leaving, was used instead of the standard C++ exception handling. Closely related to leaving is the use of the cleanup stack and two-phase construction (see Sections 6.2.2 and 6.2.3). As a consequence of this approach, class conventions were defined and named with a prefix according to the type, as described in the following:

T classes behave in the same way as the fundamental built-in data types. T stands for Type. These classes have an explicit destructor and, hence, must not contain any member data implementing destructors. T classes contain all their data internally and have no pointers, references or handles to data, unless that data is owned by another object responsible for its cleanup (see Section 6.2.2). Since Symbian v9.1, this is no longer the case. It is now possible for a T class to have a destructor to be called when the object goes out of scope.

C class objects must always be created on the heap and may contain their own pointers, as opposed to T classes. Also, they derive from the CBase class (see e32base.h). The mains of this class, which are inherited by every C class, are (i) *safe destruction*: CBase has a virtual destructor, so a CBase-derived object is destroyed properly by deletion through a base class pointer; (ii) *zero initialization*: CBase overloads operator new to zero-initialize an object when it is first allocated on the heap, and thus all member data in a CBase-derived object will be zero filled when it is first created, and there is no need for this to be done explicitly in the constructor; and (iii) *private copy constructor and assignment operators*: CBase classes declare these to prevent calling code from accidentally performing invalid copy operations. When instantiated, a C class typically needs to call code which may fail, and to avoid memory leaks you should use an idiom named two-phase construction, see Section 6.2.3.

R classes own an external resource handle, for instance a handle to a server session. They are often small and usually contain no other member data besides the resource handle. R classes may exist as class members or as local stack-based variables. Whenever you use them on the heap, for which they are intended, you must guarantee that the memory allocated is released properly (see Section 6.2.2). R objects must be made leave safe, if used in functions that may leave, by using the cleanup stack.

M classes or 'mixin' are often used in call-backs or observer classes. Thus, the M class is an abstract interface class which declares pure virtual functions and has no member data. Note that in most cases only pure virtual functions are defined for an M class.

Static classes have no prefix letter and contain only static member functions. They are used for utility classes that cannot be instantiated, e.g., User and Math. You can call their functions using the scope-resolution operator, such as User::After(200), resulting in the suspension of the currently running thread for 200 microseconds. A static class is sometimes implemented to act as a factory class.

At this point you can observe that the use of the naming convention for classes helps the creation, use and destruction of objects, and the behaviour of a user-defined class can always be matched against the Symbian OS class characteristics. Such a style ensures that even if you are not familiar with a class, you can be sure of how to instantiate an object, use it and destroy it, avoiding memory leaks.

6.1.1   Descriptors

Descriptors encapsulate strings and binary data in Symbian OS and are used to manipulate and to provide access to data. Descriptors allow efficient and secure string and binary data manipulation for memory-limited devices. They are safe since buffers can be controlled and the programmer can keep control of memory usage. Each descriptor object holds the length of the string of data it represents as well as its 'type', which identifies the underlying memory layout of the data. As descriptors hold

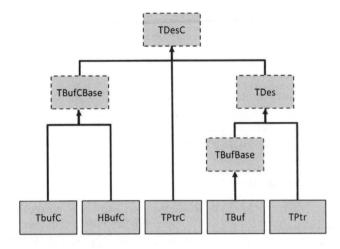

Figure 6.1 Descriptor class hierarchy.

length information, they do not need to be null terminated and can thus be used to store binary data as well as text. Descriptors can also exist in either 8-bit ASCII or 16-bit Unicode format. There are separate descriptor classes for data stored in the descriptor, named 'buffer' descriptors, or in a separate area of memory, named 'pointer' descriptors. Also, there is a further distinction between those which are stack based and those created on the heap. Further, there are descriptor types which may be accessed but not modified. These descriptor types are used for lookup and comparison, and those which may be changed by formatting, replacing or appending to the data.

As illustrated in Figure 6.1, there are a number of descriptor classes sharing the same base classes. The base classes provide common APIs for modifiable and non-modifiable descriptor operations, which are invariant to the implementation type. There are three types of descriptors:

Buffer descriptors store the data as part of the descriptor object, which typically lives on the program stack. They are used for smaller amounts of data with a fixed maximum size. TBuf<n> and TBufC<n> are buffer descriptors.

Heap descriptors store the data as part of the descriptor object, which lives on the program heap. They are used for larger amounts of data and are resizable. An example of a heap descriptor is HBufC.

Pointer descriptors contain a pointer to data, which lives elsewhere in memory. TPtr<n> and TPtrC<n> are pointer descriptors.

Observe that the trailing C indicates that the descriptor is non-modifiable. Descriptors are defined by fundamental classes TDesC and TDes implementing constant functions such as Length(), Size() and Find(). The descriptors TPtrC, TBufC and HBufC are directly derived from the TDesC class. The concrete classes add only initialization data during construction time, such as function Set(). The TDes class is derived from TDesC and implements functionalities to change data, such as Copy(), Append(), Format(), Replace() and Trim(), among others. Member data is used to store the maximum length for the descriptor.

6.1.2   Arrays

Symbian OS does not include an implementation for collections found in the Standard Template Library. Instead, it offers various classes than can be used to define static and dynamic arrays. This section describes these classes. The most basic class is TFixedArray, which is a static array class, to be used when you know at build time how many data items the array will contain.

6.2   Memory Management

As mentioned earlier, when Symbian OS was developed there was no mechanism for handling exceptions in C++. Thus, a native, lightweight exception handling mechanism, named 'leave', was introduced. Whenever an error condition or abnormal event happens, e.g. due to the lack of either main or mass memory space, leaves may occur. A leave propagates the error to a point in the calling code to be properly handled, named a TRAP harness. The developer must take into account that local resources, such as memory allocated on the heap, will be 'orphaned', therefore resulting in either memory or handle leaks. Developers working on Symbian OS must use the cleanup stack to keep track of resources to which the only pointer is an automatic variable. When a leave occurs, the cleanup stack destroys each of the resources allocated dynamically.

Note that porting standard C++ code to Symbian OS is now easier because it supports C++ standard exceptions, since Symbian OS v9. On the other hand, error handling based on leaves is still a fundamental part of Symbian OS. Thus, even though only standard C++ exceptions are used, you have to know how to mix leaves and exceptions in such a way that the ported code behaves as expected.

6.2.1   Leaves and Exception Handling

In Symbian OS the use of conventions for names is very strong, and this is also the case for leaving methods. A function name ending with L means that this function may leave, or throw an exception, such as ConstructL, for example. A function name ending with LC means that this function may leave and it will also push one item on the cleanup stack. Finally, a function name ending with LD means that this function may leave and the item that has been pushed on the stack can be released. A leave causes the execution of the active function to terminate, and the leave is propagated back through all calling functions until the first function containing a Trap() or Trapd() macro is found. An example of a leaving function is as follows:

```
1  void ProcessL() {
2      //...
3      if(error)
4          User::Leave();
5  }
```

The User::Leave() method is a static method that invokes the leave mechanism. Whenever you want to capture the exception, a catching function must be defined, for example:

```
1  void CatchingL() {
2    //...
3    ProcessL();
4    //
5  }
```

And you must set up a trap such as:

```
1  TRAPD(error, CatchingL());
2  if(error) {
3  }
```

Note that when the function leaves, it immediately returns, thus leaving currently allocated objects on the heap and leading to a memory leak. To avoid this situation you must ensure that when you leave, you clean the memory. So the leaving mechanism is strictly connected to the resource management and cleanup system, which is discussed next.

6.2.2   The Cleanup Stack

To ensure that objects allocated on the heap are properly deallocated, there is a stack, named 'cleanup stack', where objects that need to be deallocated later are pushed on. Consider the code snippet:

```
1  CDemo* demo = new CDemo;
2  OperationThatCanLeaveL();
3  delete demo;
```

If the `OperationThatCanLeaveL()` leaves, `delete demo` will never be reached, thus leaving the demo object on the heap. You must use the cleanup stack as follows:

```
1  CDemo* demo = new CDemo();
2  CleanupStack:: PushL(demo);
3  OperationThatCanLeaveL();
4  CleanupStack:: PopAndDestroy()
```

As you can see, the object that must be deallocated is pushed on a deallocation stack, the cleanup stack. If the execution is performed normally, objects are popped from the stack and destroyed automatically. In the case when the execution leaves, the cleanup is also performed in the context of leaving. The most important issue is the cleanup stack, required to recover any byte of data that can become orphaned by leaving. When an object is created by `new` or `NewL`, you have to push it on the cleanup stack if any action that follows can leave. On the other hand, if an object is created with `NewLC`, it will already be pushed on the cleanup stack at creation. When you no longer need the object, it should be destroyed. When the object is already on the cleanup stack, you should remove it from the stack with `Pop` and then delete it. You can also call `PopAndDestroy` to do both actions in a single step. Sometimes, an object may change ownership: if you put it in an array, for example, the array will take ownership and the array cleanup routine will be in charge of deleting it. In such a case, you have to pop the object from the cleanup stack to avoid double deletion. This is done through a `Pop(object)` statement. The object parameter is not required; it is provided only in order to check that you pop the expected object. It is not necessary to specify the object but it is useful to catch errors in debug build (the application panics if the popped object does not match with the parameter). In release builds, the check will be disabled. Note that the cleanup stack can be used in other ways. For instance, an R type, defining an external resource, must be closed after use. It can be pushed on the stack with `CleanupClosePushL` and when you execute `PopAndDestroy()`, the resource is closed.

6.2.3   Two-Phase Construction

Two-phase construction ensures that all objects being constructed and initialized do not leave before being stored in the cleanup. Whenever an object is constructed on the heap, the constructor is called to initialize it. Consider the case when the constructor leaves: the memory already allocated for the object as well as any additional memory the constructor may have allocated will be orphaned. In order to avoid this situation, a code within a constructor should never leave. Note that objects of C classes should be initialized using an object constructed in two phases:

1. The first phase is the standard C++ constructor which is called by the `new operator`. To avoid memory leaks the code called by this constructor should not be able to leave.

2. The second phase of the construction is where the code that is called may leave. The second-phase constructor is typically named `ConstructL`. Before it is called, the object is placed on the cleanup stack so the memory allocated for the object is leave safe. If a leave occurs, the cleanup stack calls the destructor to deallocate any resources which have already been successfully allocated and frees the memory allocated for the object itself.

A class typically provides a public static function which wraps both phases of construction, providing a simple and easy way to identify means to instantiate it (the two construction methods can then be made private or protected to avoid accidental usage). The factory function is typically called `NewL()` and it is static, so it can be called without first having an existing instance of the class.

Note that there is also a `NewLC()` function in the class `CExample`. This method is also a factory function, but its implementation leaves a pointer on the cleanup stack when it returns.

The `NewL()` factory function is implemented in terms of the `NewLC()` function rather than the other way around. This could be slightly less efficient since this would require an extra `PushL()` call to put a pointer back on the cleanup stack. Each factory function returns a fully constructed object, or leaves, either if there is insufficient memory to allocate the object (i.e. if operator `new(ELeave)` leaves) or if the second-phase `ConstructL()` function leaves for any reason. This means that, if an object is initialized entirely by two-phase construction, the class can be implemented without the need to test each member variable to see if it is valid before using it. That is, if an object exists, it has been fully constructed. Since it is not necessary to test each member variable before using it, the result is an efficient implementation.

6.2.4   Thin Templates

A thin template allows code reuse in Symbian OS to avoid code duplication. According to the thin template pattern, all functionality is provided in a non-typed base class:

```
1  class CArrayFixBase
2      {
3      IMPORT_C const TAny* At(TInt aIndex) const;
4      }
```

This base class has the real code, so it exists only once. This code is exported from its Dynamic Link Library (DLL). The base class may contain an arbitrary amount of code. A derived template class is implemented as follows:

```
1  class CArrayFix<T> : public CArrayFixBase
2      {
3      inline const T& At(TInt aIndex) const
4          {
5          return(*((const T *)CArrayFixBase::At(anIndex)));
6          }
7      }
```

Because this class uses only inline functions, it generates no extra code. However, since casting is encapsulated in the inline function, the class is type safe to its users. The derived template class is thin: it generates no new code at all. The user uses the thin templates as normal template classes. Symbian OS uses thin templates, e.g. in containers. The details of the idiom are hidden from the application programmer so they can be used like normal C++ STL (Standard Template Library) containers. An example of Symbian OS container usage is described below:

```
1  CArrayPtrSeg<TInt> avararray( 16 );
2  CArrayPtrSeg<TBool> anotherarray( 32 );
3  avararray.Insert( TInt( 20 ) ); // works fine
4  anotherarray.Insert( TInt( -1 ) ); // does not compile
5  // go to Boolean array
```

In this example, normal templates would generate separate code for the integer array and Boolean array. With thin template patterns, program code exists only once, but still there is type safety for all array types, like integer and Boolean.

6.3 Executable Files

The most commonly used Symbian OS target types are DLL, EXE and PLUGIN. An EXE runs separately and a DLL is dynamically linked into the program that loads it. DLLs are further divided into separate types. Two of the most important DLL types are shared library DLLs and polymorphic DLLs. Shared library DLLs provide a fixed API that has several entry points potentially called by the user. When used in a program, such DLLs are automatically loaded by the system. Polymorphic DLLs implement an abstract API such as a device driver or a GUI application. Other supported types are: physical and logical device drives, PDD and LDD, respectively; a static library with binary code that is included in compilation time, named LIB; and an executable which exports functions that can be used by other applications or DLLs, named EXEXP. An ECOM plug-in allows you to encapsulate functionality in a DLL and access it from multiple clients through an interface class. ECom is a client/server framework in Symbian OS that provides a service to instantiate, resolve and destroy plug-ins. UID is a 32-bit value that uniquely identifies a binary and can be as follows:

UID1 is the system-level identifier that distinguishes between EXEs and DLLs and is built into the binary by the build tools depending on the target type.

UID2 is used to differentiate between shared library and polymorphic interface DLLs. For instance, for shared libraries, UID2 is `KSharedLibraryUid(0x1000008d)`. For polymorphic DLLs, the value varies depending on their plug-in type.

UID3 uniquely identifies a file. Two executables cannot have the same UID3 value. Values must be requested from Symbian, which allocates them from a central database to ensure that each binary has a different value.

An executable program has three types of binary data: program data, read-only static data and read/write static data. EXE programs in Symbian OS are not shared. Thus, every time the program runs it gets new areas of memory allocated for all those three types of data. The only exceptions are EXEs residing in ROM. ROM-based EXEs allocate RAM only for read/write program data. In this case, the program code and read-only data are read directly from ROM. This is an optimization to save expensive RAM and improve efficiency. ROM-based code is executed in place so no copying is required.

Dynamically loaded link libraries are shared. When a DLL is loaded for the first time, it is reallocated to a particular address. When a second thread requires the same DLL, it is attached to the same copy of the code. So, no loading is required. A DLL resides in the same memory address in all threads that are using it. Symbian OS maintains reference counts, so that the DLL is unloaded when no threads are using it. Because Symbian OS DLLs are shared, they cannot have writable static data. Refer to www.symbiansigned.com as well as the Symbian Developer Library documentation in your SDK for detailed information about UIDs.

6.4   Platform Security

Symbian OS v9.1 is said to be a secure platform because of changes to the operating system to extend its security model and ensure more protection against malware or badly implemented software. The security model operates at the software level to detect and prevent unauthorized access to hardware, software and system or user data. This avoids, for example, problems with locking up the phone, compromising user data, or affecting other software or the network. The secure platform prevents programs from acting in unacceptable ways, irrespective of whether these actions are intentional or unintentional.

Whenever an application is installed, the Symbian OS installer verifies whether the application has the proper capabilities by means of a digital signature issued by a trusted authority. A capability is a privilege level assigned to every Symbian OS process, held by the kernel, that grants the trust that it will not abuse the services associated with the associated privilege. Such a signing approach avoids applications assigning to themselves capabilities prior to installation. A total of 20 capabilities are provided in Symbian OS, and must be included in the MMP file of any application. Refer to the SDK help to get more detailed information about them.

6.5   Active Objects

Symbian OS uses active objects to provide lightweight event-driven multitasking and simplify programming based on asynchronous tasks within a single thread. Therefore, active objects provide ways to make asynchronous requests, detect the completion of any task and process the results. They are used in preference to threads to reduce the overhead whenever context switches occur, as well as to use system resources efficiently. In what follows you will find details on what active objects are and how to use them.

The base class for active objects is CActive. You must create a class derived from CActive, define the method that represents the asynchronous call, and implement some base class methods that are required for the operation of active objects.

The active scheduler is a component of the system that manages the implementation of active objects and determines which active object is associated with a given event. Also, it performs the call to the active object to handle the event. Basically, there is a loop running that checks if any event of any active object ends. In this case, the scheduler invokes a method of the active object to warn about this event. This method corresponds to a RunL() of CActive that each derived class must implement. The scheduler returns to standby mode after the active object performs the response to the event. The scheduler is executed in non-pre-emptive mode. Thus, an active object cannot be interrupted in order to switch to another active object. Active objects must run to completion.

To create an active object, you must create a class derived from CActive, defined in e32base.h. CActive is an abstract class with two pure virtual functions, RunL() and DoCancel(). The following snippet defines an active object:

```
1  CMyActive class: public CActive
2  {
3    public:
4      static CMyActive * NewL ();
5      CMyActive ();
6      ~ CMyActive ();
7      InvokeAnyService void (); / / Asynchronous call
8    public:
9      // Declared in CActive
10     // It is executed when the asynchronous call is completed (mandatory)
11     RunL void ();
12     // Define what to do to cancel a call in progress (required)
13     DoCancel void ();
14     // Call to treat leaves that may occur in RunL (optional)
15     TInt RunError (TInt err);
16   private:
17     void ConstructL ();
18     TRequestStatus iStatus;
19  }
```

In order to create an active object you must execute the following steps:

1. Define functions to create the active object (ConstructL(),NewL()).

2. Register the active object to the active scheduler.

3. Define and implement the functions that represent the asynchronous calls.

4. Reset RunL(), which will be executed upon processing of the asynchronous call.

5. Reset DoCancel(), to be able to cancel an asynchronous call that is still in progress.

6. Define the destructor, which should call the Cancel() class CActive, so that all calls may be cancelled if the object is destroyed.

7. Handle exceptions and leaves, redefining the method RunError(). Note that this step is optional.

Active objects may have priorities for implementation. This property can be used if there are several active objects to be executed. The enumerated type TPriority, a member of the class CActive, defines the standard values for active objects. The class constructor CActive requires that a priority is determined so that derived classes must meet this requirement:

```
1  CMyActive: CMyActive ()
2  : CActive (CActive: EPriorityStandard)
3  {}
```

The method NewL() is responsible for constructing an instance of this object, by calling ConstructL.

The scheduler of active objects is represented by the class CActiveScheduler, and objects are registered when you call the static method Add() of this class:

```
1  CMyActive:CMyActive()
2  : CActive (CActive: EPriorityStandard)
3  {
4      CActiveScheduler::Add(this);
5  }
```

This call could also be done in ConstructL() or in NewL(). The active object is removed from the scheduler when it is destroyed, so that you do not need to do so explicitly.

Public methods provided in an active object class are used to perform calls that initiate the request to asynchronous service providers. The standard behaviour is as follows:

1. Before making the call, it is important to check whether there exists some outstanding request, because in practice each active object can have only one request in progress.

2. Submit the request, passing the iStatus member variable of TRequestStatus for the service provider asynchronously, to set this value to KRequestPending before initiating the asynchronous request.

3. If the request is successful, the method SetActive() must be called to indicate that a request is pending and the object is waiting. A call to CActive::SetActive() indicates that a request has been submitted and is currently outstanding.

When the processing related to the request finishes, the scheduler calls the RunL() method of the active object. Note that an active object class always implements the pure virtual RunL() method that is inherited from the CActive base class. The current status of the asynchronous request can be monitored through the field `iStatus` in the `TRequestStatus` object of the active object, the same that was passed to the function in the asynchronous call.

Any active object must implement the pure virtual `DoCancel()` method of the base class in order to terminate a request. This implementation should call the appropriate method that cancels a request to the asynchronous service. The `CActive::Cancel()` calls `DoCancel()` and waits for notification that the request has terminated. This method cannot leave since it can be called in the destructor of the active object. You should be aware that whenever an active object is cancelled, the method `RunL()` is not executed. Thus, the method `DoCancel()` releases resources being used when a cancellation is issued.

6.6 Error Handling

Leaves that occur in `RunL()` are treated by the method `RunError()`. The parameter represents the error code of the exception. The method should return `KErrorNone` if the error has been handled. If another value is returned, the active scheduler will be responsible for handling the error.

Note that possible errors (panics) might occur when using active objects. Such exceptions are generated by the active scheduler when a request ends but cannot identify the active object responsible to process it. Refer to the literature, such as Aubert (2008), for more details on such a situation as well as on active scheduler behaviour.

6.7 Threads

Instead of using active objects, you can use threads for multitasking – more specifically, when you are porting code from other platforms or writing code with real-time requirements. In order to manipulate threads, Symbian OS provides the class `RThread`, defining a handle to a thread. Note that the thread itself is a kernel object.

A thread is created in the suspended state and its execution initiated by calling `RThread::Resume()`. Threads are scheduled based on a pre-emptive decision mode and threads with the same priority are selected based on a round-robin policy. Threads can be suspended, and therefore no longer scheduled, by calling `RThread::Suspend()`, and can be restarted by calling `Resume()`. A call to `Kill()` or `Terminate()` normally finishes a thread and you can call `Panic()` to announce a programming error.

6.8 Qt for Symbian

6.8.1 Combining Qt and Native C++

The Qt port for Symbian was designed to provide the same level of performance as Avkon on Symbian devices. The Qt port was put on top of native Symbian and Open C libraries. As illustrated in Figure 6.2, a Symbian Qt application may access Qt libraries, Open C libraries or even native Symbian libraries. Also, the Qt libraries may access Open C libraries or native Symbian libraries.

The standard entry point of Qt application is the `main()` function. On Qt/Symbian applications the `S60Main` method implements the `E32Main()` that initializes the Symbian application UI framework, including instantiation of objects of the `CAknApplication`, `CAknDocument` and

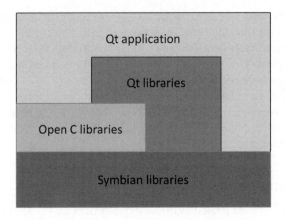

Figure 6.2 Qt/Symbian port.

CAknAppUI classes, and the creation of the control environment and active scheduler for the main thread. Finally, the S60Main method also calls the Qt main() function.

At the time of writing, the libraries ported to Symbian in the **Qt 4.6** release include: QtCore, QtGui (partially), QtNetwork, QtScript, QtSvg, QtTest, QtWebKit and QtXml.

6.8.2 Building Qt Applications in the Symbian Environment

Qt/Symbian projects use the underlying Symbian toolchain, though the projects are built in a different way. First of all, the standard Qt build tools are used as a wrapper around the Symbian tools. This means that the standard Qt project files, such as .prj and .pro, are used instead of Symbian project files. Furthermore, those files are built in the same way as a non-Symbian Qt application, using make and qmake. This integration between Symbian and Qt tool chains is illustrated in Figure 6.3.

Developers must first generate project files using the command qmake -project. As occurs for standard Qt applications, this command finds a source code file such as .h, .cpp and .ui in the current directory and builds a .pro file. Then the developer can generate the Makefile from the .pro file using the qmake command. This also generates standard Symbian build items, such as the bld.inf file, .mmp file, _reg.rss default registration file, .mk extension makefiles and .pkg package files.

The well-known Makefile also generated by qmake works as a wrapper around the standard Symbian toolchain. When the make command is executed, it calls bldmake and abld to build the Qt application. After executing the make command, and if no compilation errors were found, the binaries files are generated.

Using command-line tools may add extra levels of difficulties for some developers. An alternative to those tools is the Carbide.c++ environment. Carbide provides support for project creation, compilation, debug and UI design. To create a new Qt project, click **File→New→Qt Project** and follow the wizard.

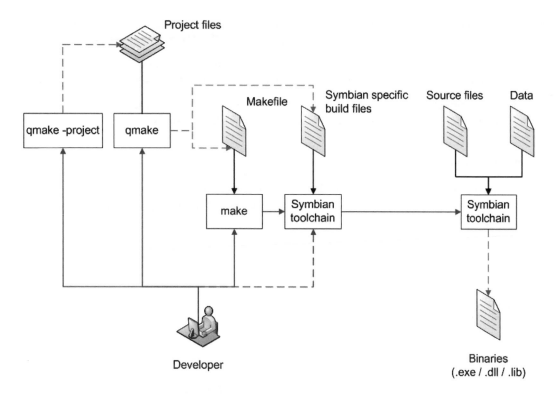

Figure 6.3 Integration of Symbian and Qt toolchain.

6.8.3 *Separating Qt and Symbian Implementations*

Besides Nokia's efforts to provide full Qt support on its devices, there are still some situations in which it is necessary to use Symbian code in order to access some functionalities of the device. One example is access to the Sensor API, such as the magnetometer API which is not yet directly supported in Qt. The main drawback is that it is necessary to separate the Symbian code explicitly from the Qt code. This is particularly true when the application can be ported to other platforms. In this way, the specific Symbian code can be easily replaced by another platform-specific code through the use of the private implementation (pimpl) pattern. The private implementations can be achieved through wrapper classes.

In what follows, we will describe how to access Symbian APIs from Qt using the pimpl pattern. The example program reads data from a magnetometer using an active object and updates the data on the device display using a `QLabel` data type. The following files are required to execute this simple task:

1. `MagnetoWidget.pro` – this is the Qt project file that `qmake` uses to generate the Makefile in order to compile the project.

2. `main.cpp` – this is the entry point of the Qt application.

3. MagnetoWidget.h and MagnetoWidget.cpp – these are the header and source files of the Qt widget that shows the magnetometer data on the display.

4. AOWrapper.h and AOWrapper.cpp – these are the header and source files of the Qt wrapper that will access platform-specific, in our case Symbian, classes.

5. AOWrapperPrivate.h and AOWrapperPrivate.cpp – these are the header and source files of the Symbian-specific classes that access the Sensor API.

The Project File

Let us start by showing the MagnetoWidget.pro file which should be modified to specify which are the Qt file classes and the platform-specific file classes. A typical Qt project file looks like the following:

```
1  TARGET = MagnetoWidget
2  QT += core \
3      gui
4  HEADERS += AOWrapper.h \
5      MagnetoWidget.h
6  SOURCES += AOWrapper.cpp \
7      MagnetoWidget_reg.rss \
8      main.cpp \
9      MagnetoWidget.cpp
```

The TARGET variable indicates the target application that will be generated. QT is used to specify the Qt libraries that should be compiled with the project. In our case, QtCore and QtGui have been added. Finally, HEADERS is used to specify the headers files and SOURCES is used to specify the source files of the project. In order to support platform-specific classes, the MagnetoWidget.pro file above should be modified by adding a section for the platform files. In our case, MagnetoWidget.pro looks like the following:

```
1  TARGET = MagnetoWidget
2  QT += core \
3      gui
4  HEADERS += AOWrapper.h \
5      MagnetoWidget.h
6  SOURCES += AOWrapper.cpp \
7      MagnetoWidget_reg.rss \
8      main.cpp \
9      MagnetoWidget.cpp
10 symbian {
11     TARGET.UID3 = 0xE5D4CBCC
12     HEADERS += AOWrapperPrivate.h
13     SOURCES += AOWrapperPrivate.cpp
14     LIBS += -lsensrvclient \
15         -lsensrvutil
16 }
```

Note that the last seven lines have been added. These lines specify which are the Symbian-specific files. Here LIBS specifies which Symbian libraries are required to compile the classes while HEADERS and SOURCES specify the header and source code files. There may be more than one platform-specific section. In this case, the compiler will decide which files should be compiled depending on the target.

The Qt Classes

The first Qt class is MagnetoWidget, which specifies the widget that will show the magnetometer date on the display. This class inherits from QtWidget and has all the UI elements of our example. Since our example is very simple, and our main purpose is to show how to separate Qt classes from Symbian-specific classes, the UI can be implemented only in the constructor of the MagnetWidget class:

```
1  MagnetoWidget::MagnetoWidget(QWidget *parent) : QWidget(parent)
2  {
3          wrapper = new AOWrapper(this);
4
5          QGridLayout *layout = new QGridLayout;
6
7          QLabel *aLabel = new QLabel(this);
8          aLabel->setAlignment(Qt::AlignHCenter);
9          aLabel->setText("Angle From Magnetic North:");
10         layout->addWidget(aLabel, 0, 0);
11
12         angle = new QLabel(this);
13         angle->setAlignment(Qt::AlignHCenter);
14         angle->setText("");
15         layout->addWidget(aLabel, 1, 0);
16
17         setLayout(layout);
18
19         connect(wrapper, SIGNAL(angle_changed(int)), angle, SLOT(setText(
               QInt)));
20 }
```

On line 3 the active object wrapper is instantiated. The AOWrapper class provides an abstraction of all platform-specific classes for accessing the Sensor API. In this way, if we are developing a program that should run on many platforms, only the AOWrapper class will be referred to by the Qt classes. On line 19, the signal angle_changed is connected to the setText slot of the Qlabel angle in which the value read from the magnetometer is shown. In short, every time the value read from the sensor changes, a signal is sent to the angle QLabel and its text is updated. The rest of the code is usual Qt:

```
1  class AOWrapper : public QObject
2  {
3          Q_OBJECT
4
```

```
 5  public: // Class constructor and destructor
 6          AOWrapper(QObject *parent = 0);
 7          virtual ~AOWrapper();
 8
 9  signals: // Signals to connect with private classes with UI
10          void angle_changed (int angle);
11
12  private: // Pointer to private classes
13          CAOWrapperPrivate *d_ptr;
14
15  private: // Friend class definitions
16      friend class CAOWrapperPrivate;
17  };
```

The AOWrapper class, which is used by MagnetoWidget, is the wrapper used to access the Symbian-specific code. It has a constructor, a destructor and a pointer to the platform-specific classes. In our case we have only one platform-specific class: d_ptr allows referring to the private class from the public class.

The public class constructor instantiates the private class object passing itself, using the this operator, to allow the private class to access its methods. Note that in the class definition above, the private classes are declared to be friend classes. This is necessary to allow the platform-specific classes to access the methods of the public Qt class. More specifically, the private classes need to access the signals defined in the public class:

```
 1  /*
 2   * AOWrapper constructor
 3   */
 4  AOWrapper::AOWrapper(QObject *parent) : QObject(parent)
 5  {
 6          d_ptr = CAOWrapperPrivate::NewL(this);
 7  }
 8
 9  /*
10   * AOWrapper destructor
11   */
12  AOWrapper::~AOWrapper()
13  {
14          delete d_ptr;
15  }
```

The Symbian-Specific Classes

The public class is responsible for providing a unique way to access platform resources from the Qt source code. Now we discuss how to implement the Symbian-specific classes to access the platform resources. Our example uses the Sensor API to get data from the magnetometer. This data can be used to implement a number of interesting applications – from a simple compass to a complete navigation system in which the map rotates on the display depending on the direction the user is moving in.

All Symbian-specific code should be implemented in the private class. If the application is being built for more than one platform, it is necessary to have specific private classes for each target platform. To allow cross-platform implementation, the source and header files for private class implementations are added to the project based on the platform.

The specific class, called CAOWrapperPrivate, accesses the Sensor API and it should be an active object that inherits from CActive. This is necessary to allow a constant update of the data read from the sensors. CAOWrapperPrivate uses the two-phase constructor of Symbian, and all objects are instantiated using the NewL method. The complete definition of the CAOWrapperPrivate class is shown below:

```
class CAOWrapperPrivate : public CActive
{
public: // Magnetometer data
        TInt iMagnetometerCalibrationLevel;
        TInt iAngleFromMagneticNorth;
        TTime iAngleFromMagneticNorthTimeStamp;

public:
        // C++ constructor
        CAOWrapperPrivate(AOWrapper *aPublicAPI = 0);

        // Cancel and destroy
        ~CAOWrapperPrivate();

        // Two-phase constructor
        static CAOWrapperPrivate* NewL(AOWrapper *aPublicAPI = 0);

        // Two-phase constructor
        static CAOWrapperPrivate* NewLC(AOWrapper *aPublicAPI = 0);

public:
        // Function for making the initial request
        void StartL(TTimeIntervalMicroSeconds32 aDelay);

private:
        // Second-phase constructor
        void ConstructL();

private:
        // Handle completion
        void RunL();

        // How to cancel me
        void DoCancel();

```

```
36      // Override to handle leaves from RunL(). Default implementation
            causes
37      // the active scheduler to panic.
38      TInt RunError(TInt aError);
39
40  // Find magnetometer sensor channel and open it
41      void CAOWrapperPrivate::FindAndOpenChannel();
42
43  // Get angle from north pole
44      void CAOWrapperPrivate::getAngleFromMagneticNorth();
45
46  // Get the calibration level
47      void CAOWrapperPrivate::getCalibrationLevel();
48
49  // Set calibration level to on/off
50      void CAOWrapperPrivate::setAutoCalibration(bool val);
51
52 private:
53      enum TAOWrapperPrivateState
54          {
55          EUninitialized, // Uninitialized
56          EInitialized, // Initialized
57          EError
58          // Error condition
59          };
60
61 private:
62      TInt iState; // State of the active object
63      RTimer iTimer; // Provides async timing service
64
65      AOWrapper *q_ptr; // Pointer to public implementation
66
67  // Channels to access magnetometer sensor data
68      CSensrvChannel* iMagnetometerSensor;
69      CSensrvChannel* iMagneticNorthSensor;
70 };
```

In order to access the Sensor API the sensrvchannel.h, sensrvchannelinfo.h, sensrvtypes.h, sensrvchannelfinder.h and sensrvdatalistener.h headers are required. The magnetometer API requires sensrvmagneticnorthsensor.h and sensrvmagnetometersensor.h also.

The CAOWrapperPrivate constructor receives a pointer to the CAOWrapper public implementation. This pointer is used later to emit a signal indicating that the data read from the sensors has changed. The constructor also initializes the public attributes. NewL and NewLC *constructors* are implemented as usual and are omitted here. This is also the same for some of the other active object methods:

```
1  CAOWrapperPrivate::CAOWrapperPrivate(AOWrapper *wrapper)
2          : CActive(EPriorityStandard), q_ptr(wrapper) // Standard priority
3  {
4          iMagnetometerCalibrationLevel = 0;
5          iAngleFromMagneticNorth = 0;
6          iAngleFromMagneticNorthTimeStamp = 0;
7  }
```

In an active object, the RunL method is executed periodically. The frequency it invokes is set by the developer. In our example, RunL opens the sensor channels on its first execution using the method FindAndOpenChannel(). From that point on, it always checks the calibration level of the sensor, and if it is too low, automatic calibration is set. When the calibration level is good, the data is recovered from the sensor and a signal is emitted (emit q_ptr->angle_changed()):

```
1  void CAOWrapperPrivate::RunL()
2  {
3          if (iState == EUninitialized) {
4
5          // In the first run should find and open sensor channels
6                  FindAndOpenChannel();
7                  iState = EInitialized;
8          } else if (iState != EError) {
9
10                 getCalibrationLevel();
11
12                 if (iMagnetometerCalibrationLevel >= 2) {
13
14                         TSensrvMagneticNorthData magNorthData;
15                         TPckg<TSensrvMagneticNorthData>  magNorthPackage(
                               magNorthData);
16                         iMagneticNorthSensor->GetData(magNorthPackage);
17
18                         iAngleFromMagneticNorth = magNorthData.
                               iAngleFromMagneticNorth;
19                         iAngleFromMagneticNorthTimeStamp = magNorthData.
                               iTimeStamp;
20
21                         emit q_ptr->angle_changed(iAngleFromMagneticNorth
                               );
22                 } else {
23
24          // If calibration level is too low, set auto calibration ON
               again
25                         setAutoCalibration(true);
26                 }
27          }
28
```

```
29      iTimer.After(iStatus, 1000000); // Set for 1 sec later
30      SetActive(); // Tell scheduler a request is active
31 }
```

Opening a channel requires execution of the following steps:

1. Instantiate a channel finder object.

2. Find the channel according to a search criterion.

3. Open the sensor channel.

In this way, it is necessary to instantiate a CSensrvChannelFinder object that is used to search for a channel using a criterion specified by a TSensrvChannelInfo object. To search for the magnetometer sensor the channel type should be set to KSensrvChannelTypeIdMagnetometerXYZAxisData, and to search for the compass sensor the channel type should be set to KSensrvChannelTypeIdMagneticNorthData. Once the desired channel is found, it can be opened using the OpenChannelL() method:

```
1  void CAOWrapperPrivate::FindAndOpenChannel()
2  {
3          // First: construct a channel finder
4      CSensrvChannelFinder* channelFinder;
5      channelFinder = CSensrvChannelFinder::NewL();
6      CleanupStack::PushL(channelFinder);
7
8      // Second: list of found channels
9      RSensrvChannelInfoList channelInfoList;
10
11     // Third: create and fill channel search criteria
12     TSensrvChannelInfo channelInfo;
13
14     // Fourth: find the channel
15     // here we look for the magnetometer channel
16     channelInfo.iChannelType =
           KSensrvChannelTypeIdMagnetometerXYZAxisData;
17     channelFinder->FindChannelsL(channelInfoList, channelInfo);
18
19     // Fifty: open the sensor channel
20     // When the channel object is created the channel info object
21     // must be an object returned by CSensrvChannelFinder::FindChannelsL
           ().
22     iMagnetometerSensor = CSensrvChannel::NewL(channelInfoList[0]);
23     CleanupStack::PushL(iMagnetometerSensor);
24     iMagnetometerSensor->OpenChannelL();
25
26     setAutoCalibration(true);
27
28     // Repeat steps 4 and 5 for the compass channel
29     channelInfo.iChannelType = KSensrvChannelTypeIdMagneticNorthData;
```

```
30      channelFinder->FindChannelsL(channelInfoList, channelInfo);
31      iMagneticNorthSensor = CSensrvChannel::NewL(channelInfoList[0]);
32      CleanupStack::PushL(iMagneticNorthSensor);
33      iMagneticNorthSensor->OpenChannelL();
34
35      CleanupStack::PopAndDestroy(channelFinder); // finder not needed any
           more
36  }
```

The Sensor API allows automatic calibration of the digital compass. However, the developer should enable it. The channel should already be open. The calibration is required to obtain more precise data from the sensors. Automatic calibration can be set on/off using the method setAutoCalibration():

```
1  void CAOWrapperPrivate::setAutoCalibration(bool val)
2  {
3          TSensrvProperty property;
4          iMagnetometerSensor->GetPropertyL(
                KSensrvPropAutoCalibrationActive,
5                                              KSensrvItemIndexNone, property);
6
7      // set auto-calibration on/off. 1 to enable, 0 to disable auto-
           calibration
8          property.SetValue(val);
9
10          iMagnetometerSensor->SetProperty(property);
11  }
```

Finally, the calibration level can be easily retrieved as shown below in the method getCalibrationLevel():

```
1  void CAOWrapperPrivate::getCalibrationLevel()
2  {
3          TSensrvProperty property;
4          iMagnetometerSensor->GetPropertyL(KSensrvPropCalibrationLevel,
                KSensrvItemIndexNone, property);
5          property.GetValue(iMagnetometerCalibrationLevel);
6  }
```

Proceeding as explained above, you can see that it is possible to separate the Symbian-specific classes, or any other platform-specific classes, from the Qt code. This isolates the platform-specific issues from the private classes, keeping the code multi-platform. Consequently, less effort is required to port it to new targets.

6.8.4   Other Issues

Error Codes

Another issue that developers should handle when building Qt/Symbian applications is the impossibility of mapping Qt error codes to Symbian error codes. This is mainly because Qt provides only class-specific error codes, but not system-wide error codes.

When an error occurs in the application, the private implementation can be used to trap a leaving method and to return such an error code to a pure Qt method that will handle the error. This can be implemented with a code such as:

```
int CAOWrapperPrivate::private_method (<list of args>)
{

    ...
    TRAPD (error, private_methodL (<list of args>););
    return error;
}
```

If something goes wrong when executing `private_methodL()`, then the error code will be trapped and handled somewhere else by showing an error message or by some other action that the developer considers more appropriate.

Allocating Memory

Developing applications for mobile devices requires some caution that is not needed when developing desktop applications. For instance, memory for personal computers is so cheap that most of the programs are not concerned with how it is used, and this is also true for most Qt applications. If the application attempts to allocate some memory and there is none available, the application is simply closed. However, this is not the scenario in developing for mobile devices, in which memory is still a limited resource.

For this reason, Symbian applications should make use of the cleanup stack to deallocate objects in the heap when an exception occurs. This is also true when building Qt/Symbian applications. When objects are created in Qt, they are stored in an object tree, making possible the automatic deletion of objects that have a parent. When an object is created, it is added to the object tree as a child of its parent. If the object is deleted, it is also removed from the tree. If its parent is deleted, then the object is automatically deleted and both are removed from the tree. This behaviour applies for objects on the heap and for objects on the stack. The only case in which an object is not automatically deleted is if it was created with *new* and has no parent. In this case the object should be explicitly deleted.

6.9 Summary

In this chapter we presented basic concepts related to Symbian OS as well as how to access the Symbian API from Qt using the pimpl pattern. The example program reads data from a magnetometer using an active object and updates the data on the device display.

Bibliography

Aubert M 2008 *Quick Recipes on Symbian OS: Mastering C++ Smartphone Development*. John Wiley & Sons, Ltd.

7

Qt for Symbian Examples

Bertalan Forstner, András Berke, Imre Kelényi, Morten V. Pedersen and Hassan Charaf

This chapter presents some examples of Qt program code for the Qt Mobility API and Qt Mobile Extensions, including a brief summary of their functionalities. The purpose of these examples is to demonstrate the features of Qt and to introduce Qt programming techniques. Developers will be able to take a closer look at the available code libraries of Qt and mobile extensions of Qt for Symbian, and obtain design ideas concerning mobile software development using the Qt for Symbian SDK. All examples can be directly downloaded from the book's web page.

7.1 Mobility API Examples

In the following we will present some examples for the use of Qt Mobility APIs. As stated above, the reader should check with our book's homepage for recent updates and extensions.

7.1.1 Displaying Messaging Accounts

The Messaging API allows the listing and manipulation of messaging accounts. If we want to send a message via a specific account, we must first acquire the account's ID. The following example widget displays a combo box with a list of the messaging accounts available on the device and emits a signal if the selected account is changed. One of the best things about messaging is that all the different types of messages can be handled via the same API, so selecting an account which is assigned to SMS and sending a text message is practically performed in the same way as selecting an email account and sending an email.

The definition of the class is as follows. There is an inner class definition for `Loader`, which encapsulates a thread responsible for querying the list of messaging accounts. This could be performed in the same thread in which the widget's methods run, but having a separate thread for the operation results in increased performance and helps prevent an unresponsive UI. The list of accounts is stored in the member variable `QMessageAccountIdList m_ids`:

```
1  class AccountsWidget : public QWidget
2  {
3  Q_OBJECT
```

```
4
5      private:
6          class Loader : public QThread
7          {
8          public:
9              Loader(AccountsWidget* parent);
10             void run();
11
12         private:
13             AccountsWidget* m_parent;
14         };
15
16     public:
17         AccountsWidget(QWidget* parent = 0);
18         QMessageAccountId currentAccount() const;
19         QString currentAccountName() const;
20         bool isEmpty() const { return m_accountsCombo->count() == 0; }
21
22     signals:
23         void accountChanged();
24
25     protected:
26         void showEvent(QShowEvent* e);
27         void hideEvent(QHideEvent* e);
28
29     private slots:
30         void load();
31         void loadStarted();
32         void loadFinished();
33
34     private:
35         void setupUi();
36         void setIds(const QMessageAccountIdList& ids);
37         QMessageAccountIdList ids() const;
38
39     private:
40         QStackedLayout* m_stackedLayout;
41         QComboBox* m_accountsCombo;
42         QLabel* m_busyLabel;
43
44         Loader m_loader;
45         mutable QMutex m_loadMutex;
46         QMessageAccountIdList m_ids;
47 };
```

The Loader overrides QThread's default run() implementation and queries the available accounts via the QMessageStore singleton. The list of accounts is then passed to the

AccountsWidget parent. A mutex is used in the setter and getter for the account IDs to prevent any undesired behaviour due to the multi-threaded execution:

```
1  AccountsWidget::Loader::Loader(AccountsWidget* parent)
2  : QThread(parent), m_parent(parent)
3  {
4  }
5
6  void AccountsWidget::Loader::run()
7  {
8          QMessageAccountIdList ids = QMessageStore::instance()->
               queryAccounts();
9          m_parent->setIds(ids);
10 }
11
12 void AccountsWidget::setIds(const QMessageAccountIdList& ids)
13 {
14         QMutexLocker mutex(&m_loadMutex);
15         m_ids = ids;
16 }
17
18 QMessageAccountIdList AccountsWidget::ids() const
19 {
20         QMutexLocker mutex(&m_loadMutex);
21         return m_ids;
22 }
```

The initialization of the class AccountsWidget is carried out by the constructor and the setupUi() method. The UI uses a QStackedLayout and QLabel to hide the combo box and display 'busy text' while the accounts are being loaded. The loader thread's started() and finished() signals are connected to the loadStarted() and loadFinished() slots:

```
1  AccountsWidget::AccountsWidget(QWidget* parent)
2  :
3  QWidget(parent),
4  m_stackedLayout(0),
5  m_accountsCombo(0),
6  m_busyLabel(0),
7  m_loader(this)
8  {
9          setupUi();
10
11         connect(&m_loader,SIGNAL(started()),this,SLOT(loadStarted()));
12         connect(&m_loader,SIGNAL(finished()),this,SLOT(loadFinished()));
13 }
14
15 void AccountsWidget::setupUi()
16 {
17         m_stackedLayout = new QStackedLayout(this);
```

```
18
19        m_accountsCombo = new QComboBox(this);
20        m_stackedLayout->addWidget(m_accountsCombo);
21        connect(m_accountsCombo,SIGNAL(currentIndexChanged(int)),this,
              SIGNAL(accountChanged()));
22
23        m_busyLabel = new QLabel("Loading...");
24        m_stackedLayout->addWidget(m_busyLabel);
25  }
```

When loading the accounts is started, QStackedLayout switches to the busy label to hide the combo box while loading is in progress.

When the loading process has finished, the list of accounts is processed by a loop, and each account name is added to the combo box:

```
1  void AccountsWidget::loadStarted()
2  {
3  #ifndef _WIN32_WCE
4        setCursor(Qt::BusyCursor);
5  #endif
6        m_stackedLayout->setCurrentWidget(m_busyLabel);
7  }
8
9  void AccountsWidget::loadFinished()
10  {
11        m_accountsCombo->clear();
12
13        QMessageAccountIdList accountIds = ids();
14
15        if(!accountIds.isEmpty())
16        {
17              for(int i = 0; i < accountIds.count(); ++i)
18              {
19                    QMessageAccount account(accountIds[i]);
20                    m_accountsCombo->addItem(QString("%1 - %2").arg(i
                          +1).arg(account.name()),account.name());
21              }
22
23              m_stackedLayout->setCurrentWidget(m_accountsCombo);
24        }
25        else
26              m_busyLabel->setText("No accounts!");
27
28  #ifndef _WIN32_WCE
29        setCursor(Qt::ArrowCursor);
30  #endif
31  }
```

The account loading process is started by calling the load() method, which uses a static variable to ensure that querying the accounts is performed only once:

```
1  void AccountsWidget::load()
2  {
3         static bool runonce = false;
4         if(!runonce)
5                 m_loader.start();
6         runonce = true;
7  }
```

Methods are also provided for getting the selected account's ID and name:

```
1  QMessageAccountId AccountsWidget::currentAccount() const
2  {
3         QMessageAccountId result;
4         if(m_loader.isFinished() && m_accountsCombo->count())
5         {
6                 int index = m_accountsCombo->currentIndex();
7                 return ids().at(index);
8         }
9
10        return result;
11 }
12
13 QString AccountsWidget::currentAccountName() const
14 {
15        if(m_loader.isFinished() && m_accountsCombo->count())
16                return m_accountsCombo->itemData(m_accountsCombo->
                       currentIndex()).toString();
17        return QString();
18 }
```

By overriding the show event handler, the widget can automatically start loading the account list when it is shown. When the widget becomes hidden, the loader is also disabled if it is running:

```
1  void AccountsWidget::showEvent(QShowEvent* e)
2  {
3         load();
4         QWidget::showEvent(e);
5  }
6
7  void AccountsWidget::hideEvent(QHideEvent* e)
8  {
9         if(m_loader.isRunning())
10                m_loader.exit();
11        QWidget::hideEvent(e);
12 }
```

7.1.2 *Displaying Recent Messages*

The following example shows how to create a widget that displays a list of recent messages. It demonstrates how to query messages from the system, how to get notifications of when messages are removed or updated, and how to use QMessageServiceAction to perform messaging-related tasks in general. The list widget shows the subject of the messages and if they are partial messages or not.

The class definition of the example widget RecentMessagesWidget is as follows. The current state of the message loading process is stored in an instance of the State enum called m_state. The displayed list items and the message IDs are tied together via QMap<QMessageId, QListWidgetItem*> m_indexMap and data is stored in each QListWidgetItem with the role MessageIdRole. This ensures that if either the list item or the message ID is present, the other can also be obtained. The class emits the signal selected(const QMessageId& messageId) when a message is selected:

```
1  class RecentMessagesWidget : public QWidget
2  {
3          Q_OBJECT
4
5  public:
6          RecentMessagesWidget(QWidget* parent = 0, unsigned int maxRecent
                  = 10);
7          ~RecentMessagesWidget();
8          QMessageId currentMessage() const;
9
10 signals:
11         void selected(const QMessageId& messageId);
12
13 protected:
14         void showEvent(QShowEvent* e);
15         void hideEvent(QHideEvent* e);
16
17 private slots:
18         void currentItemChanged(QListWidgetItem* current, QListWidgetItem
                  * previous);
19         void messagesFound(const QMessageIdList& result);
20         void stateChanged(QMessageServiceAction::State s);
21         void messageUpdated(const QMessageId& id, const QMessageStore::
                  NotificationFilterIdSet& filter);
22         void messageRemoved(const QMessageId& id, const QMessageStore::
                  NotificationFilterIdSet& filter);
23         void processResults();
24
25 private:
26         void setupUi();
27         void updateState();
28         void load();
29
```

```
30  private:
31          enum State { Unloaded, Loading, LoadFinished, Processing,
                 LoadFailed, Done };
32          static const int MessageIdRole = Qt::UserRole + 1;
33
34  private:
35          QListWidget* m_messageListWidget;
36          QLabel* m_statusLabel;
37          QStackedLayout* m_layout;
38          QMessageIdList m_ids;
39          QMap<QMessageId, QListWidgetItem*> m_indexMap;
40          unsigned int m_maxRecent;
41          QMessageServiceAction* m_service;
42          State m_state;
43          QMessageStore::NotificationFilterId m_storeFilterId;
44  };
```

After setting up the UI, the constructor connects the signals of the messaging objects to the handler slots. We are going to use a message service to get the list of messages. Message services can be accessed via QMessageServiceAction instances, in our case the member variable m_service. The messagesFound signal is emitted when a message is found by the query action and the stateChanged signal is emitted when the state of the action changes. Two signals of the QMessageStore singleton are also connected to get a notification when one of the messages is removed or updated after they have been added to the UI list.

The last line of the constructor creates and registers a filter for querying the messages. This would allow us to get only a subset of all available messages from the messaging store, but in this example the filter has no parameters, so it allows all messages. The filter must be unregistered by the widget's destructor:

```
1  RecentMessagesWidget::RecentMessagesWidget(QWidget* parent, unsigned int
       maxRecent)
2      : QWidget(parent), m_messageListWidget(0), m_statusLabel(0), m_layout(0)
         , m_maxRecent(maxRecent), m_service(new QMessageServiceAction(this)),
         m_state(Unloaded)
3  {
4          setupUi();
5          connect(m_service, SIGNAL(messagesFound(const QMessageIdList&)),
                 this, SLOT(messagesFound(const QMessageIdList&)));
6          connect(m_service, SIGNAL(stateChanged(QMessageServiceAction::
                 State)), this, SLOT(stateChanged(QMessageServiceAction::State))
                 );
7
8          //register for message update notifications
9
10         connect(QMessageStore::instance(), SIGNAL(messageUpdated(const
                 QMessageId&, const QMessageStore::NotificationFilterIdSet&)),
11             this, SLOT(messageUpdated(const QMessageId&, const
                 QMessageStore::NotificationFilterIdSet&)));
```

```
12        connect(QMessageStore::instance(),SIGNAL(messageRemoved(const
                  QMessageId&, const QMessageStore::NotificationFilterIdSet&)),
13                    this, SLOT(messageRemoved(const QMessageId&, const
                        QMessageStore::NotificationFilterIdSet&)));
14
15        m_storeFilterId = QMessageStore::instance()->
                  registerNotificationFilter(QMessageFilter());
16    }
17
18  void RecentMessagesWidget::setupUi()
19    {
20        m_layout = new QStackedLayout(this);
21
22        m_messageListWidget = new QListWidget(this);
23        m_layout->addWidget(m_messageListWidget);
24        connect(m_messageListWidget,SIGNAL(currentItemChanged(
                  QListWidgetItem*,QListWidgetItem*)),
25                    this,SLOT(currentItemChanged(QListWidgetItem*,
                        QListWidgetItem*)));
26
27        m_statusLabel = new QLabel(this);
28        m_statusLabel->setAlignment(Qt::AlignHCenter | Qt::AlignVCenter);
29        m_statusLabel->setFrameStyle(QFrame::Box);
30        m_layout->addWidget(m_statusLabel);
31    }
32
33  RecentMessagesWidget::~RecentMessagesWidget()
34    {
35        QMessageStore::instance()->unregisterNotificationFilter(
                  m_storeFilterId);
36    }
```

Querying the messages is started by the `load()` method, which issues the service action. The passed `QMessageOrdering::byReceptionTimeStamp(Qt::DescendingOrder)` ensures that the messages are returned, ordered by their timestamp.

When a message is found, the `messagesFound()` slot stores the message's ID in an array. The slot `stateChanged()` allows us to check if the service action fails or if it has completed successfully and all messages have been processed. These events are handled by the method `updateState()`:

```
1  void RecentMessagesWidget::load()
2    {
3        m_ids.clear();
4
5        if(!m_service->queryMessages(QMessageFilter(),QMessageOrdering::
                  byReceptionTimeStamp(Qt::DescendingOrder),m_maxRecent))
6                m_state = LoadFailed;
7        else
```

```
8                       m_state = Loading;
9       }
10
11      void RecentMessagesWidget::messagesFound(const QMessageIdList& ids)
12      {
13              m_ids.append(ids);
14      }
15
16      void RecentMessagesWidget::stateChanged(QMessageServiceAction::State s)
17      {
18              if(s == QMessageServiceAction::Failed)
19                      m_state = LoadFailed;
20              else if(s == QMessageServiceAction::Successful && m_state !=
                    LoadFailed)
21                      m_state = LoadFinished;
22
23              updateState();
24      }
```

The updateState() method is responsible for updating the child widgets according to the state of the messaging query action. When loading the messages has been completed, it starts processing them by calling processResults()), which puts the messages into the list widget. Only the subject of the messages is displayed, but the font of the list entry also indicates if the message is a partially or fully downloaded message.

Note that newItem->setData(MessageIdRole, id.toString()) is used to store the message ID in the list item's data model so that it can be obtained when the widget is selected in the UI:

```
1       void RecentMessagesWidget::updateState()
2       {
3               switch(m_state)
4               {
5                       case Unloaded:
6                       {
7                               m_statusLabel->setText(QString());
8                               m_layout->setCurrentWidget(m_statusLabel);
9                       }
10                      break;
11                      case Loading:
12                      {
13                              m_statusLabel->setText("Loading...");
14                              m_layout->setCurrentWidget(m_statusLabel);
15                      }
16                      break;
17                      case LoadFinished:
18                      {
19                              if(m_ids.isEmpty())
20                              {
```

```
21              m_statusLabel->setText("Finished. No
                   messages.");
22              m_layout->setCurrentWidget(m_statusLabel)
                   ;
23          }
24          else
25          {
26              m_state = Processing;
27              updateState();
28              processResults();
29          }
30      }
31      break;
32  case Processing:
33          m_layout->setCurrentWidget(m_messageListWidget);
34      break;
35  case LoadFailed:
36      {
37          m_statusLabel->setText("Load failed!");
38          m_layout->setCurrentWidget(m_statusLabel);
39      }
40      break;
41  }
42
43  #ifndef _WIN32_WCE
44      if(m_state == Loading || m_state == Processing)
45          setCursor(Qt::BusyCursor);
46      else
47          setCursor(Qt::ArrowCursor);
48  #endif
49  }
50
51  void RecentMessagesWidget::processResults()
52  {
53      if(!m_ids.isEmpty())
54      {
55          QMessageId id = m_ids.takeFirst();
56          QMessage message(id);
57
58          QListWidgetItem* newItem = new QListWidgetItem(message.
               subject());
59          newItem->setData(MessageIdRole,id.toString());
60          QFont itemFont = newItem->font();
61          bool isPartialMessage = !message.find(message.bodyId()).
               isContentAvailable();
62          itemFont.setItalic(isPartialMessage);
63          newItem->setFont(itemFont);
64          m_messageListWidget->addItem(newItem);
```

```
65              m_indexMap.insert(id,newItem);
66              m_messageListWidget->update();
67              QTimer::singleShot(100,this,SLOT(processResults()));
68         }
69     else
70     {
71              m_state = Done;
72              updateState();
73     }
74 }
```

After querying the messages has been done and listing them in the list widget, it is still possible that one of them is updated or removed. This is why the messageUpdated() and messageRemoved() slots were connected in the constructor. These update the list by either removing or updating the list entry for the given message:

```
1  void RecentMessagesWidget::messageUpdated(const QMessageId& id, const
      QMessageStore::NotificationFilterIdSet& filter)
2  {
3          if(!filter.contains(m_storeFilterId) || m_state == Loading || !id
            .isValid() || !m_indexMap.contains(id))
4                  return;
5
6          //update the pertinent entry to reflect completeness
7
8          QListWidgetItem* item = m_indexMap.value(id);
9          if(item)
10         {
11                 QMessage message(id);
12                 bool partialMessage = !message.find(message.bodyId()).
                      isContentAvailable();
13                 QFont itemFont = item->font();
14                 itemFont.setItalic(partialMessage);
15                 item->setFont(itemFont);
16         }
17 }
18
19 void RecentMessagesWidget::messageRemoved(const QMessageId& id, const
      QMessageStore::NotificationFilterIdSet& filter)
20 {
21         if(!filter.contains(m_storeFilterId) || m_state == Loading || !id
            .isValid() || !m_indexMap.contains(id))
22                 return;
23
24         QListWidgetItem* item = m_indexMap.value(id);
25         if(item)
26         {
27                 int row = m_messageListWidget->row(item);
```

```
28          QListWidgetItem* item = m_messageListWidget->takeItem(row
               );
29          m_indexMap.remove(id);
30          delete item;
31      }
32      m_ids.removeAll(id);
33  }
```

To allow further use of the widget besides displaying a list of the subjects of the most recent messages, a signal is emitted when one of them is selected. Another widget can connect to the signal and, for instance, display the body of the selected message.

The ID of the selected message can also be accessed by currentMessage():

```
1  void RecentMessagesWidget::currentItemChanged(QListWidgetItem*,
     QListWidgetItem*)
2  {
3      if(m_state != Processing || m_state != Loading)
4          emit selected(currentMessage());
5  }
6
7  QMessageId RecentMessagesWidget::currentMessage() const
8  {
9      QMessageId result;
10
11     if(QListWidgetItem* currentItem = m_messageListWidget->
           currentItem())
12         result = QMessageId(currentItem->data(MessageIdRole).
               toString());
13
14     return result;
15 }
```

The widget's load and hide event handlers ensure that loading of the messages is started when the widget becomes visible and stopped when it goes out of sight:

```
1  void RecentMessagesWidget::showEvent(QShowEvent* e)
2  {
3      if(m_state == Unloaded)
4          load();
5
6      updateState();
7
8      QWidget::showEvent(e);
9  }
10
11 void RecentMessagesWidget::hideEvent(QHideEvent* e)
12 {
13     if(m_state == Loading || m_state == Processing)
14     {
```

```
15              m_service->cancelOperation();
16              m_state = Unloaded;
17              m_ids.clear();
18          }
19
20      QWidget::hideEvent(e);
21  }
```

7.1.3 Service Framework

In this section we will demonstrate the functionality of the service framework by developing a simple 'helloworld' service example. We will also show how we can use the service framework to register and discover our new service on the Symbian device. To demonstrate that our new service can be found on the device, you can use the ServiceBrowser example found in the Mobility API examples folder. The example shown here will only cover a small part of the functionalities available in the service framework. However, it demonstrates the most fundamental functionality needed to develop new service plug-ins. For more information on the service framework you should consult the Qt Mobility documentation.

Creating a Service Plug-in

The first step we need to perform is to create our service plug-in code. First we must define a plug-in interface using the `QServicePluginInterface` class. The service framework will interact with our service though the plug-in interface. The listing below shows the interface declaration from `helloworldplugin.h`:

```
1
2  #include <QObject>
3  #include <QServicePluginInterface.h>
4
5  using namespace QtMobility;
6
7  class HelloWorldPlugin : public QObject,
8                          public QServicePluginInterface
9  {
10     Q_OBJECT
11     Q_INTERFACES(QtMobility::QServicePluginInterface)
12  public:
13     QObject* createInstance(const QServiceInterfaceDescriptor& descriptor
                ,
14                          QServiceContext* context,
15                          QAbstractSecuritySession* session);
16  };
```

As seen in the above listing, we must implement the pure virtual factory function `createInstance()` from `QServicePluginInterface`. This function is called by the service framework to instantiate our plug-in. The parameters of the createInstance() function will allow us to support, for example, multiple service implementations in a single plug-in and to check whether the client has sufficient permissions to load the plug-in. However, in this example we ignore the parameters passed and simply return a new instance of our 'helloworld' plug-in as shown in the listing below (defined in helloworldplugin.cpp):

```
1  #include <QServiceInterfaceDescriptor.h>
2  #include <QAbstractSecuritySession.h>
3  #include <QServiceContext.h>
4
5  #include "helloworldplugin.h"
6  #include "helloworld.h"
7
8  QObject* HelloWorldPlugin::createInstance(const
       QServiceInterfaceDescriptor& /*descriptor*/,
9                                           QServiceContext* /*context*/,
10                                          QAbstractSecuritySession* /*
                                                 session*/)
11 {
12     return new HelloWorld(this);
13 }
14
15 Q_EXPORT_PLUGIN2(serviceframework_helloworldplugin, HelloWorldPlugin)
```

The Q_EXPORT_PLUGIN2(targetname, pluginname) macro exports the plug-in class targetname for the plug-in specified by pluginname. The value of pluginname should correspond to the TARGET specified in the service plug-in's project file as we will see later.

We have now implemented the necessary plug-in handling code. The next step is to define the actual plug-in behaviour in the HelloWorld class. The following listings show the implementation of the class declaration and definition:

```
1  #include <QObject>
2
3  class HelloWorld : public QObject
4  {
5      Q_OBJECT
6  public:
7      HelloWorld(QObject *parent = 0);
8
9  public slots:
10     void sayHello();
11 };
```

```
1  #include <QtCore>
2
3  #include "helloworld.h"
4
5  HelloWorld::HelloWorld(QObject *parent)
6      : QObject(parent)
```

```
7  {
8  }
9
10 void HelloWorld::sayHello()
11 {
12     qDebug() << "Hello World :)";
13 }
```

As seen above, the actual plug-in code is very simple and for it to work we only have to fulfil a few rules. Our plug-in code must be derived from QObject and we must implement the functions invoked by the service framework using the Qt signal and slot mechanism. This allows the service framework to use the Qt meta-system to detect which function can be invoked in our plug-in, in this case the sayHello() function.

Now we define the project file, which will tell the Qt build system how to build our plug-in. The .pro file is shown in the Listing below:

```
1  TEMPLATE = lib
2  CONFIG += plugin
3
4  INCLUDEPATH += C:\Qt\qt-mobility-src-1.0.0-tp\src\serviceframework
5
6  HEADERS += helloworldplugin.h
7  SOURCES += helloworldplugin.cpp
8
9  HEADERS += helloworld.h
10 SOURCES += helloworld.cpp
11
12 TARGET = serviceframework_helloworldplugin
13
14 CONFIG += mobility
15 MOBILITY = serviceframework
16
17 LIBS += -lQtServiceFramework_tp
18
19 symbian {
20
21     load(data_caging_paths)
22     pluginDep.sources = serviceframework_helloworldplugin.dll
23     pluginDep.path = $$QT_PLUGINS_BASE_DIR
24     DEPLOYMENT += pluginDep
25
26     TARGET.EPOCALLOWDLLDATA = 1
27 }
```

Note that we are linking against QtServiceFramework_tp, where _tp is appended, since we are using the technology preview of the service framework. You should now be able to build the plug-in using your preferred Qt for Symbian IDE. Also note that you first have to make sure that you have a built version of the Service Framework Library supplied in the Qt Mobility API source package. On Symbian the service framework will run as a server, therefore you first need to build and install the service framework server before you can use the application on a device. After installing this server and our new service plug-in on our device, we still need to make the service framework discover our new plug-in. This is done by adding a service description file in XML to the service manager running on our device. The XML file for the 'helloworld' plug-in can be found in the service_installer_helloworld folder of the example source code. This folder also contains a small Symbian application needed to register the our 'helloworld' service on the device. The registration phase is a little different on the Symbian platform than for other platforms and is documented here: `http://doc.trolltech.com/qtmobility-1.0-tp/` `service-framework-on-symbian.html`.

7.2 Qt for Symbian and Mobile Extension Examples

Now we look at the mobile extension examples. The examples cover the basics of Qt, networking, XML and Symbian-specific features such as sensors, audio, messaging, a camera and localization. Even though there are Mobility APIs available, developers might want to use the extensions in order to be more flexible. All of these small demonstration programs were implemented and tested using the Carbide.c++ 2.0.2 IDE and Qt for Symbian release 4.6.0.

7.2.1 Basic Widgets Example

The first example demonstrates how the standard Qt widgets can be arranged on a simple GUI to realize some basic input functionality. Let us assume that our task is to create a simple form named `MyMoviesForm`, on which the user could provide information about recently seen movies. This could be useful, e.g. when we are working on a mobile client application of a movie ranking site. Our form will contain some simple input fields; a line edit widget for entering the title of the movie; a group of radio buttons to let the user specify the language of the movie; and a checkbox, which the user could use to recommend watching the film. Further, we need a list of the movies already added, a button to add a new movie with the given details, and another one to remove any of the previously added list items. To build an input form as described, we could just use the Qt Designer Editor in Carbide.c++. In that case, we just have to drag and drop the widget items from the widgets box and arrange them in a layout. As you might have read in a previous chapter, it is also possible to create the form manually in program code, by instantiating widget and layout items and linking them in the desired way. However, in all the examples of this chapter we will follow the first way. The main advantage of creating the UI in this way is that in this case we can focus the source code on program functionality.

After adding all the necessary widget items, we can just simply right-click on the form and select the option *Lay out/Lay out in a grid*. Using this command simplifies the arrangement of form items (see Figure 7.1). Our next task is to customize some of the widgets' properties like the shown text, the title of the window or the C++ name of the widget instance. We can easily perform this using the Qt C++ Property Editor.

After all the necessary modifications, we can use the Build Project command from the Project menu to generate the code that describes the form's UI exactly as designed

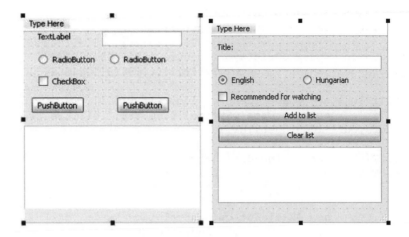

Figure 7.1 Illustration of Qt Designer's auto layout function.

with the Qt tool. The listing of the source code for the generated class (naming schema: Ui_<name_of_the_main_widget>Class.cpp) is as follows:

```
1
2  QT_BEGIN_NAMESPACE
3
4  class Ui_MyMoviesFormClass
5  {
6  public:
7      QWidget *centralwidget;
8      QGridLayout *gridLayout;
9      QLabel *lblTitle;
10     QLineEdit *editTitle;
11     QRadioButton *radioEng;
12     QRadioButton *radioHun;
13     QCheckBox *chkRecommend;
14     QPushButton *btnAdd;
15     QPushButton *btnClear;
16     QListWidget *listMovies;
17     QMenuBar *menubar;
18     QStatusBar *statusbar;
19
20     void setupUi(QMainWindow *MyMoviesFormClass)
21     {
22         if (MyMoviesFormClass->objectName().isEmpty())
23         MyMoviesFormClass->setObjectName(
24         QString::fromUtf8("MyMoviesFormClass"));
25
26         centralwidget = new QWidget(MyMoviesFormClass);
```

```
27    centralwidget->setObjectName(
28    QString::fromUtf8("centralwidget"));
29
30    gridLayout = new QGridLayout(centralwidget);
31    gridLayout->setObjectName(QString::fromUtf8("gridLayout"));
32
33    lblTitle = new QLabel(centralwidget);
34    lblTitle->setObjectName(QString::fromUtf8("lblTitle"));
35    gridLayout->addWidget(lblTitle, 0, 0, 1, 2);
36
37    editTitle = new QLineEdit(centralwidget);
38    editTitle->setObjectName(QString::fromUtf8("editTitle"));
39    gridLayout->addWidget(editTitle, 1, 0, 1, 2);
40
41    radioEng = new QRadioButton(centralwidget);
42    radioEng->setObjectName(QString::fromUtf8("radioEng"));
43    radioEng->setChecked(true);
44    gridLayout->addWidget(radioEng, 2, 0, 1, 1);
45
46    radioHun = new QRadioButton(centralwidget);
47    radioHun->setObjectName(QString::fromUtf8("radioHun"));
48    gridLayout->addWidget(radioHun, 2, 1, 1, 1);
49
50    chkRecommend = new QCheckBox(centralwidget);
51    chkRecommend->setObjectName(QString::fromUtf8("chkRecommend"));
52    gridLayout->addWidget(chkRecommend, 3, 0, 1, 2);
53
54    btnAdd = new QPushButton(centralwidget);
55    btnAdd->setObjectName(QString::fromUtf8("btnAdd"));
56    gridLayout->addWidget(btnAdd, 4, 0, 1, 2);
57
58    btnClear = new QPushButton(centralwidget);
59    btnClear->setObjectName(QString::fromUtf8("btnClear"));
60    gridLayout->addWidget(btnClear, 5, 0, 1, 2);
61
62    listMovies = new QListWidget(centralwidget);
63    listMovies->setObjectName(QString::fromUtf8("listMovies"));
64    gridLayout->addWidget(listMovies, 6, 0, 1, 2);
65
66    MyMoviesFormClass->setCentralWidget(centralwidget);
67    menubar = new QMenuBar(MyMoviesFormClass);
68    menubar->setObjectName(QString::fromUtf8("menubar"));
69    menubar->setGeometry(QRect(0, 0, 262, 21));
70    MyMoviesFormClass->setMenuBar(menubar);
71    statusbar = new QStatusBar(MyMoviesFormClass);
72    statusbar->setObjectName(QString::fromUtf8("statusbar"));
73    MyMoviesFormClass->setStatusBar(statusbar);
74
```

```
75        retranslateUi(MyMoviesFormClass);
76
77        QMetaObject::connectSlotsByName(MyMoviesFormClass);
78    } // setupUi
79
80    void retranslateUi(QMainWindow *MyMoviesFormClass)
81    {
82        MyMoviesFormClass->setWindowTitle(
83        QApplication::translate(
84        "MyMoviesFormClass", "My Movies", 0,
85        QApplication::UnicodeUTF8));
86
87        lblTitle->setText( QApplication::translate("MyMoviesFormClass", "
              Title:", 0, QApplication::UnicodeUTF8));
88        radioEng->setText(QApplication::translate("MyMoviesFormClass", "
              English", 0, QApplication::UnicodeUTF8));
89        radioHun->setText(QApplication::translate("MyMoviesFormClass", "
              Hungarian", 0, QApplication::UnicodeUTF8));
90        chkRecommend->setText(
91        QApplication::translate("MyMoviesFormClass",
92        "Recommended for watching", 0, QApplication::UnicodeUTF8));
93        btnAdd->setText(QApplication::translate("MyMoviesFormClass", "Add
              to list", 0, QApplication::UnicodeUTF8));
94        btnClear->setText(QApplication::translate("MyMoviesFormClass", "
              Clear list", 0, QApplication::UnicodeUTF8));
95        Q_UNUSED(MyMoviesFormClass);
96    } // retranslateUi
97
98 };
99
100 namespace Ui {
101    class MyMoviesFormClass: public Ui_MyMoviesFormClass {};
102 } // namespace Ui
103
104 QT_END_NAMESPACE
```

As you may have noticed, the UI class consists of two functions, one named setupUi (called by the MyMoviesForm widget's constructor in order to lay out the enclosed widget items) and the other retranslateUi (called by the UI class itself).

Note that in the rest of the examples of this chapter we will dispense with listing the generated UI header source code. However, in most cases we will assume that such a header file exists.

After studying the UI source code, we can look at the declaration of the MyMoviesForm widget:

MyMoviesForm.h

```
1 #include <QtGui/QMainWindow>
2
3 //including the generated layout header
4 #include "ui_MyMoviesForm.h"
```

```
 5
 6  class MyMoviesForm : public QMainWindow
 7  {
 8      Q_OBJECT
 9
10  public:
11          MyMoviesForm(QWidget *parent = 0);
12      ~MyMoviesForm();
13
14  private:
15      Ui::MyMoviesFormClass ui;
16
17  private slots:
18          void on_btnAdd_clicked();
19
20  };
```

The class MyMoviesForm is derived from QMainWindow, which means that it is responsible for providing a framework for building the application's UI. Its declaration consists of the standard constructor/destructor methods, the previously mentioned UI class, and the declaration of a private slot called on_btnAdd_clicked(), which we are going to use for implementing the click event handler function for the Add button. The reason for this naming method is that Qt can detect the slot declaration named on_<widget_name>_<widget_signal_name>() and it connects the particular signal automatically to this specially named slot. Hence, there is no need to call Qt's connect() method in source code.

Finally, here is the implementation of MyMoviesForm:

```
 1  #include "MyMoviesForm.h"
 2
 3  MyMoviesForm::MyMoviesForm(QWidget *parent)
 4      : QMainWindow(parent)
 5  {
 6          //calling the previously mentioned setupUi() function
 7          ui.setupUi(this);
 8
 9          //connecting: btnClear pressed -> clear list
10          connect(ui.btnClear, SIGNAL(clicked()),
11                                  ui.listMovies, SLOT(clear()));
12
13          //No need for connecting Add button's clicked() signal to
14          //on_btnAdd_clicked() private slot explicitly.
15          //Qmake will do that automatically.
16  }
17
18  void MyMoviesForm::on_btnAdd_clicked()
19  {
20          //btnAdd clicked.
21          //adding new item to the listwidget if there's any
```

```
22        if(!ui.editTitle->text().isEmpty()) {
23            QString title = ui.editTitle->text();
24
25            QString lang = ui.radioEng->isChecked() ?
26                                    QString("ENG") :
27                                    QString("HUN");
28
29            QString recommend = ui.chkRecommend->isChecked() ?
30                                    QString(" *") :
31                                    QString("");
32
33            ui.listMovies->addItem(
34                        title + " (" + lang + ")" + recommend);
35
36            ui.editTitle->setText("");
37        }
38  }
39
40  MyMoviesForm::~MyMoviesForm()
41  {
42
43  }
```

In the source code above we have implemented the window's constructor function, in which we call the UI arranger function, and connect the 'Clear list' button's `clicked()` signal to the list's `clear()` slot. By connecting these entities, we achieve our aim that all the list items will be deleted on the button click event.

Below the constructor method, you can find the implementation of the click event handler slot. Its functionality is quite simple: it gathers the information that the user has provided using the input widget items, creates its string representation and adds the string to the list as a new item.

In Figure 7.2 you can see what the layout of the widget example application would look like when running on a mobile device.

7.2.2 Background Worker Class

The following example will demonstrate how to use Qt's signals and slots mechanism to design and implement a communication interface between your UI widgets and business logic classes. The source code basically consist of two classes: a `QMainWindow` object, which is responsible for building the UI and handling user input, and an additional Qt object called `MyWorkerClass`, which will implement the business method of this demo application.

In consideration of the purpose of this demonstration, the worker class will implement only a very simple functionality: it takes an integer as an input parameter and raises it to the second, third and fourth power, and then makes the result available to its caller as a `QString` object:

```
1  #ifndef MYWORKERCLASS_H_
2  #define MYWORKERCLASS_H_
3
```

Figure 7.2 The widget example running on the Symbian emulator.

```
4  #include <QObject>
5  #include <QString>
6
7  class MyWorkerClass : public QObject
8  {
9          Q_OBJECT
10
11 public:
12          MyWorkerClass(QObject* = 0);
13          virtual ~MyWorkerClass();
14 const static int ERROR_NOT_A_POSITIVE_NUMBER=1;
15
16 public slots:
17          void doWork(int param);
18
19 signals:
20          void onFinished(const QString& result);
21          void onError(int errCode);
22 };
23
24 #endif /* MYWORKERCLASS_H_ */
```

The MyWorkerClass declaration consists of standard constructor/destructor functions, an integer constant used as an error code value, and a public slot named doWork() which may be attached to a signal or simply called directly by the UI class, in order to start the processing of the given input value.

Further, this class also declares two signals, one named `onFinished()`, emitted when the processing is over, and the second named `onError()`, emitted only in the case of a processing error. Following this design, the worker class can notify its caller if any exception occurs during processing (which, in this case, could only be an error caused by an invalid input parameter). Note that the accessibility of signals as opposed to slots cannot be controlled by the developer; all the signals are public and therefore available for connecting to any `QObject`'s slot.

It is important to declare the class as a `QObject` class, and to use the `Q_OBJECT` directive as well, in order take advantage of using Qt's signals and slots mechanism.

The implementation of the worker class follows:

```
1   #include "MyWorkerClass.h"
2   #include <math.h>
3
4   MyWorkerClass::MyWorkerClass(QObject* parent)
5   : QObject(parent) {}
6
7   MyWorkerClass::~MyWorkerClass() {}
8
9   void MyWorkerClass::doWork(int param)
10  {
11          //class business functionality
12
13          if(param<1) {
14                  //input is 0 or negative --> emitting error signal
15          emit onError(ERROR_NOT_A_POSITIVE_NUMBER);
16  }
17
18          else {
19                  //processing input
20                  QString retval=QString::number(param);
21                  for(int i=2;i<5;i++) {
22                          retval+=", "+QString::number(pow(param,i));
23                  }
24
25                  //finished, passing the result string
26                  emit onFinished(retval);
27          }
28  }
```

As previously mentioned, the `doWork()` method implements the processing of the input parameter, and in the case of success it emits the `onFinished()` signal, passing the string value as a result. If an invalid parameter was given, it emits the `onError()` signal without calculating the result or emitting any other signal.

After implementing the background working class, the next step is to design a `QMainWindow` UI class consisting of Qt widgets able to offer a testing environment for the previously presented calculator functionality. The UI design of this class might look like that described in Table 7.1.

Table 7.1   UI design of the worker class example.

QLabel	Shows 'Value:' string
QLineEdit *editValue*	Input value
QPushButton *btnGet*	Starts calculation
QLabel	Shows 'Results:' string
QLabel *lblResults*	Shows result value
Spacer	For layout alignment purposes

outcome

As mentioned in the first example of this chapter, the source code describing the UI is always generated by the IDE, so there is no need to construct the desired layout by writing its source code. It is only necessary to include the generated UI header file and declare an instance of it as a variable, as listed above in the source code for the Qt window of this example:

```
1
2  #ifndef WORKERCLASSEXAMPLE_H
3  #define WORKERCLASSEXAMPLE_H
4
5  #include <QtGui/QMainWindow>
6  #include "MyWorkerClass.h"
7
8  //including the generated layout header
9  #include "ui_WorkerClassExample.h"
10
11 class WorkerClassExample : public QMainWindow
12 {
13     Q_OBJECT
14
15 public:
16     WorkerClassExample(QWidget *parent = 0);
17     ~WorkerClassExample();
18
19 private:
20     Ui::WorkerClassExampleClass ui;
21
22     //worker class instance
23     MyWorkerClass *workerClass;
```

```
24
25  private slots:
26          void onWorkerError(int error);
27          void on_btnGet_clicked();
28
29  };
30
31  #endif // WORKERCLASSEXAMPLE_H
```

Apart from the standard constructor/destructor methods, the WorkerClassExample window declares two slots: onWorkerError(), which will be connected to the worker class onError() signal; and on_btnGet_clicked(), which – as previously mentioned – will be connected automatically by Qt to the btnGet button widget's clicked signal. Note that no slot is declared in the window class for the worker class onFinished() signal. The reason for this is because the signal will be connected directly to the label widget's setText() slot.

Finally, here is the implementation of the WorkerClassExample window:

```
1   #include "WorkerClassExample.h"
2
3   WorkerClassExample::WorkerClassExample(QWidget *parent)
4       : QMainWindow(parent)
5   {
6           ui.setupUi(this);
7
8   //instantiate workerclass
9           workerClass = new MyWorkerClass(this);
10
11          //connecting the workerclass signals
12          connect(workerClass, SIGNAL(onError(int)),
13                  this , SLOT(onWorkerError(int)));
14
15          connect(workerClass, SIGNAL(onFinished(const QString&)),
16                  ui.lblResults , SLOT(setText(const QString& )));
17  }
18
19  void WorkerClassExample::on_btnGet_clicked()
20  {
21          //slot direct method call
22          workerClass->doWork(ui.editValue->text().toInt());
23  }
24
25  void WorkerClassExample::onWorkerError(int error)
26  {
27
28  //showing error message instead of the result value
29  QString errStr("Unknown");
30
31          if(error==MyWorkerClass::ERROR_NOT_A_POSITIVE_NUMBER)
```

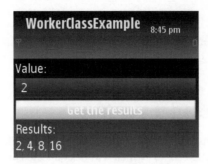

Figure 7.3 The worker class example running on the Symbian emulator.

```
32              errStr=QString("Not a positive number.");
33
34          ui.lblResults->setText("Error: "+errStr);
35  }
36
37  WorkerClassExample::~WorkerClassExample() {}
```

Figure 7.3 shows how the worker class example application would behave when running on a mobile device.

7.2.3   Bouncing Ball

The following 'bouncing ball' example will introduce to you the Qt Graphics Library and use of the QTime class. It also demonstrates how overriding some of the QWidget's functions can be used to get notifications about key events.

You might already be familiar with the 'bouncing ball' demo application. It displays a filled circle moving constantly within the bounds of a window, which is actually a single QWidget descendant. To implement such behaviour, we override the QWidget::paintEvent() protected method, which will be called when the framework asks the widget to repaint itself. When this event occurs, the contents of the widget have already been erased, so we can draw on the blank surface of the widget itself. To draw the desired shapes, we can use the services of the QPainter class. This object is responsible for implementing all the low-level drawing functions, including drawing different kinds of shapes, manipulating the drawing parameters and setting up matrix transformations.

To paint a moving ball, we modify the drawn shape's position and repaint the container widget repetitively. We can easily achieve this using Qt's QTimer class. By connecting a timer's timeout() signal – which will be emitted at constant intervals – to the widget's update() slot, we can ensure that the window will be repainted periodically.

In the following example we will realize the bouncing ball application in the way explained above; in addition to implementing some supplementary user input handling functions, to demonstrate Qt's key event handling approach, we will make the ball movable by pressing the direction keys as well.

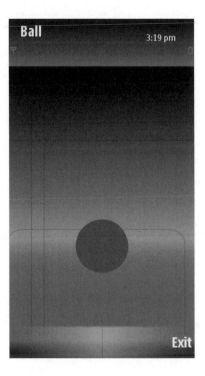

Figure 7.4 Screenshot of the bouncing ball example.

We can accomplish this by overriding the QWidget::keyPressEvent() method and changing the position of the ball by a constant distance depending on the direction key chosen.

The header file and the implementation of the described Qt application called BallExample are listed below; the ball painted on the widget's surface is shown in Figure 7.4:

BallExample.h:

```
1  #ifndef BALL_H
2  #define BALL_H
3
4  #include <QtGui/QWidget>
5  #include <QTimer>
6  #include <QPaintEvent>
7  #include <QPainter>
8  #include <QColor>
9  #include <QTime>
10 #include <QRect>
11 #include <QPoint>
12 #include <QString>
13
```

```
14  //including the generated layout header
15  //the UI consists of a single full-screen QWidget
16  #include "ui_Ball.h"
17
18  class BallExample : public QWidget
19  {
20      Q_OBJECT
21
22  public:
23      BallExample(QWidget *parent = 0);
24      ~BallExample();
25
26  protected:
27      void paintEvent(QPaintEvent* event);
28      void keyPressEvent (QKeyEvent * event);
29
30  private:
31      Ui::BallClass ui;
32      QTimer* timer;
33
34      //the ball's properties
35      QPoint r; //position
36      QPoint v; //velocity
37      const int D; //diameter
38  };
39
40  #endif // BALL_H
```

BallExample.cpp:

```
1   #include "BallExample.h"
2
3   BallExample::BallExample(QWidget *parent)
4       : QWidget(parent), D(100)
5   {
6       ui.setupUi(this);
7
8       //initialize timer, and connect it to the widget's update slot
9       //calling update forces the widget to repaint itself
10      timer = new QTimer(this);
11      connect(timer, SIGNAL(timeout()), this, SLOT(update()));
12
13      //start emitting
14      timer->start(50);
15
16      //initialize the ball's properties
17      r.setX(this->width() / 2);
18      r.setY(this->height() / 2);
19      v.setX(10);
```

```
20          v.setY(10);
21
22  }
23
24  BallExample::~BallExample()
25  {
26
27  }
28
29  void BallExample::paintEvent(QPaintEvent* event)
30  {
31
32          //move ball
33          r+=v;
34          if(r.x() < 0) {
35                  r.setX(0);
36                  v.setX(-v.x());
37          }
38          else if(r.x() > width()-D) {
39                  r.setX(width()-D);
40                  v.setX(-v.x());
41          }
42
43          if(r.y() < 0) {
44                  r.setY(0);
45                  v.setY(-v.y());
46          }
47          else if(r.y() > height()-D) {
48                  r.setY(height()-D);
49                  v.setY(-v.y());
50          }
51
52          //draw ball in its new position
53          QPainter painter(this);
54          QColor color(255, 0, 0);
55          painter.setBrush(color);
56          painter.setPen(color);
57          painter.setRenderHint(QPainter::Antialiasing);
58          painter.translate(r.x(),r.y());
59          painter.drawEllipse(0,0,D,D);
60
61  }
62
63  void BallExample::keyPressEvent(QKeyEvent * event)
64  {
65          //handling keypress event
66          //the direction keys move the ball in addition to
67          //moving caused by timer events
```

Table 7.2   UI design of the softkey example.

QLabel	Shows 'Cut . . . ' string
QLineEdit *editCut*	Source text box
QLabel	Shows 'And . . . ' string
QLineEdit *editPaste*	Destination text box
Spacer	For layout alignment purposes
outcome	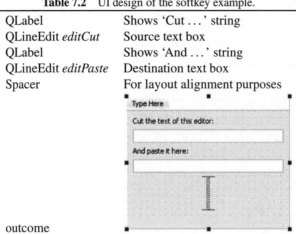

```
68    int key=event->key();
69    if(key == Qt::Key_Left) r+=QPoint(-40,0);
70    else if(key == Qt::Key_Right) r+=QPoint(40,0);
71    else if(key == Qt::Key_Down) r+=QPoint(0,40);
72    else if(key == Qt::Key_Up) r+=QPoint(0,-40);
73    }
```

7.2.4   Options Menu

Mobile applications often have to deal with a complex UI containing many input widgets and command buttons. However, it might not be the best idea to display all the necessary fields on the tiny screen that mobile devices often have. In order to realize a more user friendly environment, applications could use the device's softkey menu to display command actions as simple menu items.

In the following demonstration we take a brief look at the method of creating softkey menu items and change their behaviour dynamically. The example itself is a Qt form consisting of two line editors. The menu items will implement some basic cut and paste functionality. Selecting the 'cut' menu item will result in clearing the first text box's content and copying it to a private string variable. The 'paste' menu item will be responsible for inserting the stored string value into the second text editor. The UI design of the example is presented in Table 7.2.

Note that the widget itself does not contain any command buttons; all the program functionality can be reached, as the following program code demonstrates.

At first, you might look at the declaration file of the softkey demo application. There menu items are represented as instances of the QAction class, which provides a general UI action handled by menus and toolbars. In our case, it will be added to the menu bar of the Qt window, which is actually shown as the softkey menu on the Symbian mobile platform. In our demo application the softkey menu will be made context sensitive. This means that the menu items will be displayed only if the corresponding line editor focuses on the input. The Qt approach for handing various sets of input events (including focus changes) is the use of the filter pattern. This means that programmers can handle certain events by overriding the parent widget's eventFilter(QObject*, QEvent*) method and implement the desired functionality based on the received parameters, which identify the event type occurring and the object that triggered it. If your reimplementation of the event filter method returns true, the handled event will be 'filtered out', i.e. will not be passed to any other registered event filter. Otherwise, if you were not going to handle a certain event, you could just pass it to the filter method of the parent class.

In our case, the event filter method will handle only the FocusIn event of the two line editors, in order to decide which item will be shown in the options menu bar of the device. This behaviour can be achieved by setting the corresponding QAction's enabled Boolean property to 'true' and the other ones to 'false'.

After this brief summary of Qt's input handling, we list below the header file and the implementation of the Qt application that realizes the previously described cut and paste functionality:

Softkeys.h:

```
1  #ifndef SOFTKEYS_H
2  #define SOFTKEYS_H
3
4  #include <QtGui/QMainWindow>
5  #include <QAction>
6  #include "ui_Softkeys.h"
7
8  class Softkeys : public QMainWindow
9  {
10     Q_OBJECT
11
12 public:
13     Softkeys(QWidget *parent = 0);
14     ~Softkeys();
15
16 private:
17     Ui::SoftkeysClass ui;
18
19     //menu actions
20     QAction* cutAction;
21     QAction* pasteAction;
22
23     //represents the clipboard
24     QString clipboard;
25     //focus handling filter
26     bool eventFilter(QObject *obj, QEvent *event);
27
28     //cut & paste functionality
29     void cutEditor();
30     void pasteEditor();
31 };
```

```
32
33 #endif // SOFTKEYS_H
```

Softkeys.cpp:

```
1 #include "Softkeys.h"
2
3 Softkeys::Softkeys(QWidget *parent)
4     : QMainWindow(parent)
5 {
6         ui.setupUi(this);
7
8         //register actions on the menu
9         cutAction=menuBar()->addAction(
10 "Cut", this, SLOT(cutEditor()));
11         cutAction->setEnabled(false);
12
13         pasteAction=menuBar()->addAction(
14 "Paste", this, SLOT(pasteEditor()));
15         pasteAction->setEnabled(false);
16
17         //register event filters for focus event notifications
18         ui.editCut->installEventFilter(this);
19         ui.editPaste->installEventFilter(this);
20
21         //clear clipboard
22         clipboard="";
23
24 }
25
26 bool Softkeys::eventFilter(QObject *obj, QEvent *event)
27 {
28
29     if (event->type() == QEvent::FocusIn) {
30                 //focus in event received
31                 if(obj->objectName()=="editCut") {
32                         cutAction->setEnabled(true);
33                         pasteAction->setEnabled(false);
34                         return true;
35                 }
36                 else if(obj->objectName()=="editPaste") {
37                         cutAction->setEnabled(false);
38                         pasteAction->setEnabled(true);
39                         return true;
40                 }
41         return true;
42
43     } else {
44         //passing the event to the parent
```

```
45        return QMainWindow::eventFilter(obj, event);
46    }
47  }
48  void Softkeys::cutEditor()
49  {
50        //cut functionality
51        clipboard=ui.editCut->text();
52        ui.editCut->setText("");
53  }
54
55  void Softkeys::pasteEditor()
56  {
57        //paste functionality
58        ui.editPaste->setText(clipboard);
59  }
60
61  Softkeys::~Softkeys(){}
```

Figure 7.5 shows what the context-sensitive softkey menu would look like on a Symbian mobile device.

7.2.5 Website Downloader

In this section one of the most commonly used classes in the QtNetwork module, called QNetworkAccessManager, is introduced. The network class library offers various classes that allow the developer to write low-level networking applications, (encrypted) socket servers/clients, and high-level protocol-specific clients like FTP or HTTP. Generally, QNetworkAccessManager is responsible for posting requests and receiving replies. It offers a simple and useful interface, so – after an instance of this class has been created – the developer could use its methods to launch requests over the network (represented as QNetworkRequest objects) without a huge effort. The returned object is a QNetworkReply instance, which class might be useful in order to obtain all the downloaded data and metadata.

Our application that demonstrates the QNetworkAccessManager functionality will be a simple website downloader. Its user interface (see Table 7.3) will consist of an input field for providing the URL, a button for starting the request, a progress bar that allows the user to monitor the download process, and a QLabel widget on which the response will be displayed.

In the case of implementing a website downloader application, we should use a simple HTTP get request. The easiest way to do this is by using the QNetworkAccessManager::get() function. The request runs asynchronously, which means that all the important events (successfully downloaded fragment, error detected in processing, etc.) are reported via signals, which are offered by the QNetworkReply object. In the following example, we connect two of these to our QMainWindows slots: finished() (emitted when a request is finished); and downloadProgress() (emitted to indicate the current progress of the download, which can be very useful if we want to show a progress bar on our window). When the get request is finished, we can use the QNetworkReply::readAll() method to access the downloaded content and place it on the surface of a widget, e.g. a QLabel.

Figure 7.5 The softkeys example running on the Symbian emulator.

The header file and the implementation of the website downloader application are listed below. Note that, before compiling and running an application that uses a class from the QtNetwork module, it is important to add the network to the project descriptor (usually called <MainWindowName>.pro) file:

Downloader.h:

```
1
2  #ifndef DOWNLOADER_H
3  #define DOWNLOADER_H
4
5  #include <QtGui/QMainWindow>
6  #include <QNetworkAccessManager>
7  #include <QNetworkRequest>
8  #include <QNetworkReply>
9  #include "ui_Downloader.h"
10
11 class Downloader : public QMainWindow
12 {
13     Q_OBJECT
```

Table 7.3   UI design of the website downloader example.

QLineEdit *editUrl*	Input value
QPushButton *btnDownload*	Starts downloading
QProgressBar *prgDownload*	Progress bar
QLabel *lblContent*	Displays result
Spacer	For layout alignment purposes

outcome	

```
14
15  public:
16      Downloader(QWidget *parent = 0);
17      ~Downloader();
18
19  private:
20      Ui::DownloaderClass ui;
21      QNetworkAccessManager netManager;
22
23  private slots:
24      void on_btnDownload_clicked();
25      void on_download_finished();
26      void on_receivingProgress(qint64 done, qint64 total);
27
28  };
29
30  #endif // DOWNLOADER_H
```

Downloader.cpp:

```
1  #include "Downloader.h"
2  #include <QUrl>
3
4  Downloader::Downloader(QWidget *parent)
5      : QMainWindow(parent)
6  {
7      ui.setupUi(this);
8  }
9
```

```
10  void Downloader::on_btnDownload_clicked()
11  {
12      ui.progressDownload->setValue(0);
13
14      //sets the requested url
15      QUrl url("http://" + ui.editUrl->text());
16      QString hostname = url.encodedHost();
17      QString file = url.encodedPath();
18
19      //init request
20      QNetworkRequest request;
21      request.setUrl(url);
22
23      QNetworkReply *reply = manager->get(request);
24      connect(reply, SIGNAL(finished()), this, SLOT(on_download_finished())
            );
25      connect(reply, SIGNAL(downloadProgress(qint64, qint64)),
26              this, SLOT(on_receivingProgress(qint64, qint64)));
27  }
28
29  void Downloader::on_download_finished()
30  {
31      QByteArray resp=http->readAll();
32      ui.lblContent->setText(QString(resp.data()));
33  }
34
35  void Downloader::on_receivingProgress(qint64 done, qint64 total)
36  {
37      ui.progressDownload->setMaximum(total);
38      ui.progressDownload->setValue(done);
39  }
40
41  Downloader::~Downloader()
42  {
43
44  }
```

In Figure 7.6 you can see how the HTTP client could be used to download and display simple HTML pages.

7.2.6 Stored Settings

In the following example, the XML processing library of the Qt platform is introduced. Our demo application's source code will explain how the QXmlStreamReader class can be used for parsing an input configuration written in XML. This reader class handles the input XML document as a stream of tokens, just like the standard SAX parser. As you will see, the difference is that, while the SAX parsing is based on asynchronous call-back functions, QXmlStreamReader supports

Figure 7.6 Downloading a simple website using the demo application.

loop-based reading, which can be helpful, for example, in implementing recursive processing by splitting the parsing logic of different types of elements into different methods (demonstrated in the FriendsApp example below).

Our very first XML parser function will be responsible for processing the following XML file input:

```
<?xml version="1.0"?>
<settings>
  <label>
    <red value="255" />
    <green value="0" />
    <blue value="0" />
  </label>
  <slider value="22" />
  <time value="02:02:22" />
</settings>
```

As you may have guessed, this structure describes the predefined set values of a few widget items: the background colour of a `QLabel`, the value of a `QSlider`, and the displayed time of a `QTimeEdit`, respectively. The parsing function `parseSettings()` will be called immediately after setting up the UI, and then the read values will be applied by calling the `applySettings()` function. Therefore, if the input document is well formed, after launching the application a set of widgets (presented in Table 7.4) containing the read values will be shown.

The header file and the implementation of the stored settings example are listed as follows:

Table 7.4   UI design of the stored settings example.

QLabel *lblHeader*	Will change its background colour
QSlider *horizontalSlider*	Will change its value
QTimeEdit *timeEdit*	Will change its displayed time
Spacer	For layout alignment purposes
outcome	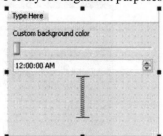

StoredSettings.h:

```
1
2  #ifndef STOREDSETTINGS_H
3  #define STOREDSETTINGS_H
4
5  #include <QtGui/QMainWindow>
6  #include <QFile>
7  #include <QXmlStreamReader>
8  #include "ui_StoredSettings.h"
9
10 class StoredSettings : public QMainWindow
11 {
12     Q_OBJECT
13
14 public:
15         StoredSettings(QWidget *parent = 0);
16     ~StoredSettings();
17
18 private:
19         Ui::StoredSettingsClass ui;
20         //variables storing processed input
21         QColor settingsColor;
22         int settingsSlider;
23         QTime settingsTime;
24
25         void parseSettings(const QString& data);
26         void applySettings();
27 };
28
29 #endif // STOREDSETTINGS_H
```

StoredSettings.cpp:

```cpp
1  #include "StoredSettings.h"
2
3  StoredSettings::StoredSettings(QWidget *parent)
4      : QMainWindow(parent)
5  {
6    ui.setupUi(this);
7
8    // Open input file
9    QFile settingsFile("stored_settings.xml");
10
11   if (settingsFile.open(QIODevice::ReadOnly)) {
12 parseSettings(settingsFile.readAll().data()); //parse input file
13       settingsFile.close();
14 applySettings();
15   }
16
17 }
18
19 void StoredSettings::parseSettings(const QString& data)
20 {
21   QXmlStreamReader reader(data);
22   bool inSettingsTag=false;
23   bool inLabelTag=false;
24
25   while (!reader.atEnd()) {
26     reader.readNext(); //read next token
27
28     if (reader.tokenType() == QXmlStreamReader::StartElement) {
29
30       if (reader.name() == "settings") {
31 inSettingsTag=true;
32       }
33       else if(reader.name() == "label" && inSettingsTag) {
34         inLabelTag=true;
35       }
36       else if(reader.name() == "red" && inLabelTag) {
37         int value= reader.attributes()
38                 .value("value").toString().toInt();
39         settingsColor.setRed(value);
40       }
41       else if(reader.name() == "green" && inLabelTag) {
42         int value= reader.attributes()
43                 .value("value").toString().toInt();
44         settingsColor.setGreen(value);
45       }
46       else if(reader.name() == "blue" && inLabelTag) {
```

```
47          int value= reader.attributes()
48                      .value("value").toString().toInt();
49          settingsColor.setBlue(value);
50        }
51      else if(reader.name() == "slider" && inSettingsTag) {
52          settingsSlider= reader.attributes()
53                      .value("value").toString().toInt();
54        }
55      else if(reader.name() == "time" && inSettingsTag) {
56          QString timeString= reader.attributes()
57                      .value("value").toString();
58          settingsTime=QTime::fromString(timeString);
59        }
60    } //startElement
61
62    else if (reader.tokenType() == QXmlStreamReader::EndElement) {
63
64      if(reader.name() == "settings")
65          inSettingsTag=false;
66
67      else if(reader.name() == "label")
68          inLabelTag=false;
69
70    }
71
72  } //while !reader.atEnd()
73
74 }
75
76 void StoredSettings::applySettings()
77 {
78
79        ui.lblHeader->setStyleSheet("QLabel { background-color: "+
80                        settingsColor.name()+"; }");
81
82        ui.horizontalSlider->setValue(settingsSlider);
83        ui.timeEdit->setTime(settingsTime);
84
85 }
86 StoredSettings::~StoredSettings() {}
```

In Figure 7.7 you can see what the Qt form looks like after parsing and processing the input XML file.

7.2.7   FriendsApp

Our very last example application concerning Qt XML and networking functions might seem a little more complex, since it uses most of the previously introduced modules of the Qt framework in order

Figure 7.7 The stored settings example running on the Symbian emulator.

to realize a mobile client application of a basic social networking site. FriendsApp was meant to be created only for demonstration purposes, so its functionality will cover just the simplest use cases of such an application, which are the login process and the downloading of a user's friend list.

The communication process between the server and the mobile client is realized via HTTP get requests completed with the proper query parameters describing the requested operation. The server's response is always an XML document, thus `QXmlStreamReader` will be used in order the process the pulled data bundle.

First, we take a closer look at the communication process. The login query looks as follows (note that in our demonstration the password is transmitted as plain text; advanced authentication methods or ciphering are not included):

```
http://<server_address>/?function=login&email=
<user_login_email>&password=<password>
```

The server's response for a login request in which valid credentials are provided is as follows:

```
<friendsapp>
  <login>
    <id>user_id</id>
    <sid>session_id</sid>
    <email>user_login_email</email>
    <nick>user_nick</nick>
  </login>
</friendsapp>
```

The most important node of this login response is the session ID (tagged `<sid>`), since all the FriendsApp functions provided by the server – fetching or managing friends, searching, sending text messages, etc. – require (sometimes among others) a valid `sid` as an input parameter.

If the given username or password is incorrect, an error message will be transmitted as a login response. The scheme of such a message is as follows:

```
<friendsapp>
  <message code="error_code"/>
<friendsapp>
```

After a successful login procedure, our client application can request any of the server's functions. Since the FriendsApp Qt example will cover the function of downloading and displaying current friends and friend request, we can examine the request format and the response of the friend fetching function. The request's URL is:

```
http://<server_address>/?function=get_friends&sid
=<session_id>
```

The response XML document consists of several <friend> nodes (which represent the actual friends of the user) and <friend_request> nodes (which supply information about incoming friend requests). The scheme of this list is as follows:

```
<friendsapp>
  [<friend>
     <userid>friend_user_id</userid>
     <nick>friend_nick</nick>
     <email>friend_login_email</email>
     <lastlogin>time_of_last_login</lastlogin>
   </friend> *]
  [<friend_request>
     <userid> user_id</userid>
     <nick>nick</nick>
     <email> login_email</email>
     <lastlogin>time_of_last_login</lastlogin>
   </friend_request> *]
</friendsapp>
```

In case of any processing error (wrong sid supplied by the client, server application cannot connect to database, etc.), the previously mentioned error message will be transmitted, containing the exact cause of the error.

After examining the communication process between the server and the client application, finally we can implement the network client class of our application which will be responsible for managing the active session, handling network requests and processing responses using the previously introduced SAX parser. This class, called FriendClient, offers two public methods in order to launch the previously described request: login(QString username, QString password) and fetchFriendList(). Note in the source code of these functions that the network requests use http://www.example.com/friendsapp/ as the address of the FriendsApp server. Note also that implementing and running the application with this address will result in a login error as the site example.com does not really exist. This means that in order to test the functionality of an application based on the following demonstration, you will have to create and a run a server that will respond to the requests sent from the mobile client of FriendsApp.

The implementation of the class utilizes the singleton design pattern. As you will see, the UI of our client application consists of more Qt windows, so we could use the singleton pattern in order to reach exactly the same instance of the FriendClient class from every Qt window.

The communication process between the FriendClient and the widget classes can be realized by connecting the client's signals to the corresponding slots of widget objects. Some of these signals relate to the login procedure (loginSuccess() and loginFailed(int errorcode)) and some to the significant events of the friend list downloading process:

- fetchStarted() – Emitted at the start of the parsing process.
- friendFetched(QString) – Emitted after successfully parsed friend or friend request element. The string parameter represents the downloaded friend.
- fetchError() – Emitted in case an error has been raised during the downloading or parsing process.
- fetchFinished(int numberOfFriendsFetched) – Emitted at the end of parsing.

The header file and the implementation of the FriendClient class based on the described behaviour are listed below:

FriendClient.h:

```
1  #ifndef FRIENDSCLIENT_H_
2  #define FRIENDSCLIENT_H_
3
4  #include <QObject>
5  #include <QNetworkAccessManager>
6  #include <QNetworkReply>
7  #include <QUrl>
8  #include <QString>
9  #include <QXmlStreamReader>
10 #include <QDateTime>
11
12
13 class FriendsClient : public QObject
14 {
15         Q_OBJECT
16
17 public:
18 virtual ~FriendsClient();
19
20 static FriendsClient* getInstance(); //singleton instance
21         void login(QString, QString); //starts the login procedure
22         void fetchFriendList(); //starts friend list fetching
23
24
25 private:
26         FriendsClient();
27         static FriendsClient* instance;
28
29 //access managers for network requests
30         QNetworkAccessManager loginAccessManager;
31         QNetworkAccessManager downloadAccessManager;
32
33 //stores sid after a successful login
```

```
34        QString sessionId;
35
36        //XML parser functions
37        void parseLoginReply(const QString &);
38        void parseFetchReply(const QString &);
39        QString parseFriend(QXmlStreamReader &reader,
40        QString elementName, bool showLastSeen);
41
42 private slots:
43        //callback for finished network request
44        void on_loginRequestFinished(QNetworkReply*);
45        void on_fetchRequestFinished(QNetworkReply*);
46
47 signals:
48
49 //signals emitted to notify the login UI class
50 void loginSuccess();
51        void loginFailed(int);
52        //signals emitted to notify the friend list UI class
53 void fetchStarted();
54        void friendFetched(QString);
55        void fetchError();
56        void fetchFinished(int);
57
58 };
59
60 #endif /* FRIENDSCLIENT_H_ */
```

   FriendClient.cpp:

```
1 #include "FriendsClient.h"
2
3 FriendsClient* FriendsClient::instance=0;
4
5 FriendsClient::FriendsClient()
6 {
7   //connecting network signals to private slots
8   connect(&loginAccessManager, SIGNAL(finished(QNetworkReply*)),
9                 this, SLOT(on_loginRequestFinished(QNetworkReply*)));
10   connect(&downloadAccessManager, SIGNAL(finished(QNetworkReply*)),
11                 this, SLOT(on_fetchRequestFinished(QNetworkReply*)));
12 }
13
14 FriendsClient::~FriendsClient() {}
15
16 FriendsClient* FriendsClient::getInstance()
17 {
18   //static functions, provides the singleton instance
19   if(!instance) instance=new FriendsClient();
```

```
20   return instance;
21 }
22
23 void FriendsClient::login(QString username, QString password)
24 {
25   //starts a login request with the supplied parameters
26   QUrl url("http://www.example.com/friendsapp/");
27   url.addEncodedQueryItem("function", "login");
28   url.addEncodedQueryItem("email", username.toUtf8());
29   url.addEncodedQueryItem("password", password.toUtf8());
30   loginAccessManager.get(QNetworkRequest(url));
31 }
32
33 void FriendsClient::fetchFriendList()
34 {
35   //starts a fetch request with the supplied parameters
36   QUrl url("http://www.example.com/friendsapp/");
37   url.addEncodedQueryItem("function", "get_friends");
38   url.addEncodedQueryItem("sid", sessionId.toUtf8());
39   downloadAccessManager.get(QNetworkRequest(url));
40 }
41
42
43
44 void FriendsClient::on_loginRequestFinished(QNetworkReply* reply)
45 {
46   //reads the login response
47   if (!reply->error()) {
48     QByteArray resp=reply->readAll();
49     parseLoginReply(resp.data());
50   }
51   else {
52     emit loginFailed(0);
53   }
54
55 }
56
57 void FriendsClient::on_fetchRequestFinished(QNetworkReply* reply)
58 {
59   //reads the login response
60   if (!reply->error()) {
61     QByteArray resp=reply->readAll();
62     parseFetchReply(resp.data());
63   }
64   else {
65     emit fetchError();
66   }
67
```

```
68  }
69
70  void FriendsClient::parseLoginReply(const QString &respString)
71  {
72
73    QXmlStreamReader reader(respString);
74
75    while (!reader.atEnd()) {
76      reader.readNext();
77      if (reader.tokenType() == QXmlStreamReader::StartElement) {
78        if (reader.name() == "message") {
79            //got a message answer
80            //login failed for some reason
81            //(wrong username, password, etc.)
82            QString param=reader.attributes().value("code").toString();
83            emit loginFailed(param.toInt());
84            return;
85        }
86          else if(reader.name() == "sid") {
87            //got a valid sessionId
88            sessionId=reader.readElementText();
89            emit on_loginSuccess();
90            return;
91          }
92      }
93    } //while !reader.atEnd()
94
95    emit loginFailed(1);
96
97  }
98
99  void FriendsClient::parseFetchReply(const QString &respString)
100 {
101    QXmlStreamReader reader(respString);
102
103    int fetchedItemCount=0;
104    emit fetchStarted();
105
106    while (!reader.atEnd()) {
107      reader.readNext();
108      if (reader.tokenType() == QXmlStreamReader::StartElement) {
109        if (reader.name() == "friend") {
110            QString text=parseFriend(reader, QString("friend"), true);
111            emit friendFetched(text);
112            fetchedItemCount++;
113          }
114        else if (reader.name() == "friend_request") {
115            QString text=parseFriend(reader, QString("friend_request"),
```

```
116                          false);
117                  emit friendFetched(text+" wants to be your friend");
118                  fetchedItemCount++;
119              }
120          }
121      }
122
123      emit fetchFinished(fetchedItemCount);
124
125  }
126
127
128  QString FriendsClient::parseFriend(QXmlStreamReader &reader, QString
        elementName, bool showLastSeen)
129  {
130      QString nick("");
131      QDateTime lastSeen;
132
133      reader.readNext();
134      while(!(reader.tokenType() == QXmlStreamReader::EndElement &&
135              reader.name() == elementName)) {
136
137          if(reader.tokenType() == QXmlStreamReader::StartElement) {
138              if(reader.name() == "nick") {
139                  nick=reader.readElementText();
140              }
141              else if(reader.name() == "lastlogin") {
142                  int seconds=reader.readElementText().toInt();
143                  lastSeen=QDateTime::fromTime_t(seconds);
144              }
145          }
146          reader.readNext();
147      }
148
149      return showLastSeen ?
150          nick+ " (last seen "+lastSeen.toString("hh:mm dd.MM.yy")+")" :
151          nick;
152  }
```

After implementing the background worker class, the next step is to design the two necessary Qt forms. The first one is to provide a conventional login surface, consisting of widgets such as username and password editor. After a successful login, the second form should appear on the screen, on which the user can download the friend list and examine the results.

The UI design and the implementation of these form widgets called LoginForm (see Table 7.5) and FriendListForm (see Table 7.6) follow. The source code does not contain any unfamiliar code snippet, after studying the preceding examples of this chapter, hence we will dispense with a detailed description of the following classes. After studying the implementation of the FriendsApp

Table 7.5   UI design of the FriendsApp login window.

QLabel *lblLogin*	Status report
QLineEdit *editEmail*	Login username
QLineEdit *editPassword*	Login password
QPushButton *btnLogin*	Start login
Spacer	For layout alignment purposes
outcome	

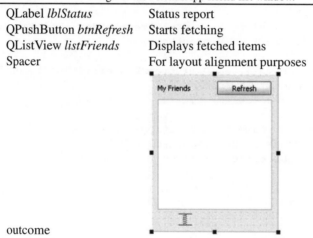

Table 7.6   UI design of the FriendsApp friend list window.

QLabel *lblStatus*	Status report
QPushButton *btnRefresh*	Starts fetching
QListView *listFriends*	Displays fetched items
Spacer	For layout alignment purposes
outcome	

UI classes, you might take a look at the screenshots of the running application. Figure 7.8 shows an unsuccessful login attempt on the login form, while in Figure 7.9 you can see how the downloaded XML representation of the contact data will be transformed into a friend list on the GUI:

LoginForm.h:

```
1  #ifndef LOGINFORM_H
2  #define LOGINFORM_H
3
4  #include <QtGui/QMainWindow>
5  #include "ui_LoginForm.h"
6  #include "FriendsClient.h"
7
```

Figure 7.8 Unsuccessful login attempt in the FriendsApp login form.

Figure 7.9 The XML representation of a downloaded friend list and the corresponding screenshot.

```
8   class LoginForm : public QMainWindow
9   {
10      Q_OBJECT
11
12  public:
13          LoginForm(QWidget *parent = 0);
14      ~LoginForm();
15
16
17  private slots:
18          void on_btnLogin_clicked();
19
20  public slots:
```

```
21        void on_loginSuccess();
22        void on_loginFailed(int);
23
24 private:
25        FriendsClient *friendsClient;
26     Ui::LoginFormClass ui;
27
28 };
29
30 #endif // LOGINFORM_H
```

LoginForm.cpp:

```
1  #include "LoginForm.h"
2  #include <QByteArray>
3  #include <QString>
4  #include "FriendListForm.h"
5
6  LoginForm::LoginForm(QWidget *parent)
7      : QMainWindow(parent)
8  {
9    ui.setupUi(this);
10
11   friendsClient=FriendsClient::getInstance();
12
13   connect(friendsClient, SIGNAL(on_loginSuccess()),
14                          this, SLOT(on_loginSuccess()));
15   connect(friendsClient, SIGNAL(on_loginFailed(int)),
16                          this, SLOT(on_loginFailed(int)));
17
18 }
19
20 LoginForm::~LoginForm () {}
21
22
23 void LoginForm::on_btnLogin_clicked()
24 {
25   friendsClient->login(ui.editEmail->text(),ui.editPassword->text());
26 }
27
28 void LoginForm::on_loginSuccess()
29 {
30   FriendListForm* fl=new FriendList();
31   fl->showMaximized();
32 }
33
34 void LoginForm::on_loginFailed(int messageCode)
35 {
36   ui.lblLogin->setText("Login failed: " +
```

```
37              QString::number(messageCode));
38  }
```

FriendListForm.h:

```
1  #ifndef FRIENDLISTFORM_H
2  #define FRIENDLISTFORM_H
3
4  #include <QtGui/QWidget>
5  #include <QString>
6  #include "ui_FriendListForm.h"
7  #include "FriendsClient.h"
8
9  class FriendListForm : public QWidget
10  {
11      Q_OBJECT
12
13  public:
14      FriendListForm(QWidget *parent = 0);
15      ~FriendListForm();
16
17  private:
18      Ui::FriendListFormClass ui;
19      FriendsClient* friendsClient;
20
21  private slots:
22      void on_btnRefresh_clicked();
23
24  public slots:
25      void on_fetchError();
26      void on_fetchFinished(int);
27      void on_friendFetched(QString);
28
29  };
30
31  #endif // FRIENDLISTFORM_H
```

FriendListForm.cpp:

```
1  #include "FriendListForm.h"
2
3  FriendListForm::FriendListForm(QWidget *parent)
4      : QWidget(parent)
5  {
6    ui.setupUi(this);
7
8    friendsClient=FriendsClient::getInstance();
9
10    connect(friendsClient, SIGNAL(fetchStarted()),
11                ui.listFriends, SLOT(clear()));
```

```
12    connect(friendsClient, SIGNAL(fetchFinished(int)),
13                   this, SLOT(on_fetchFinished(int)));
14    connect(friendsClient, SIGNAL(fetchError()),
15                   this, SLOT(on_fetchError()));
16    connect(friendsClient, SIGNAL(friendFetched(QString)),
17                   this, SLOT(on_friendFetched(QString)));
18
19  }
20
21  FriendListForm::~FriendListForm() {}
22
23  void FriendListForm::on_btnRefresh_clicked()
24  {
25    friendsClient->fetchFriendList();
26  }
27
28
29  void FriendListForm::on_fetchFinished(int itemcount)
30  {
31    ui.lblStatus->setText("Fetched "+QString::number(itemcount)+
32      " item(s)");
33    if(!itemcount) {
34      ui.listFriends->addItem("You have no friends.");
35    }
36  }
37
38  void FriendListForm::on_friendFetched(QString friendStr)
39  {
40    ui.listFriends->addItem(friendStr);
41  }
42
43  void FriendListForm::on_fetchError()
44  {
45    ui.lblStatus->setText("Error while fetching");
46  }
```

```xml
<friendsapp>
<friend>
  <userid>54</userid>
  <nick>Elemer</nick>
  <email>me2@abc</email>
  <lastlogin>1250416017</lastlogin>
</friend>
<friend>
  <userid>55</userid>
  <nick>Joseph</nick>
  <email>me3@abc</email>
```

```
    <lastlogin>1250416040</lastlogin>
  </friend>
  <friend>
    <userid>56</userid>
    <nick>Cornelius</nick>
    <email>me4@abc</email>
    <lastlogin>1250425144</lastlogin>
  </friend>
  <friend_request>
    <userid>57</userid>
    <nick>Paula</nick>
    <email>me5@abc</email>
    <lastlogin>1251483051</lastlogin>
  </friend_request>
</friendsapp>
```

7.2.8   Sensor API

In addition to standard Qt class libraries – which were developed originally for use in a desktop environment – mobile extensions for Qt for Symbian offer you a varied set of APIs in order to provide native support for technologies that are available for mobile devices. These technologies include messaging, location-based services, a camera, an acceleration meter, and so on. The interfaces allow developers to reach the Symbian mobile technologies without a huge effort, since, with the extension pack, they can implement the whole application in Qt program code. Note that the extension classes are not part of the Qt for Symbian SDK. In order to access their services, you have to obtain the Mobile Extensions for Qt for Symbian pack, and install it on your development environment. Check the documentation on mobile extensions for more details.

The following short examples will demonstrate the functionality of one of these extension libraries, the Sensor API. Mobile devices are often crafted with built-in sensor hardware. Symbian OS provides a programming interface that gives developers access to the sensor services, and with the mobile extensions these sensors are also available in Qt. The first example program code demonstrates how easy it is to register an orientation change listener with the XQDeviceOrientation class. The second example covers the topic of the acceleration meter API (accessible through the XQAccelerationSensor class), which is trickier to use, since instead of the Qt signals and slots mechanism it uses the filter pattern. The reason for this is because acceleration sensor events are triggered so often that they cannot be handled using the standard signals and slots interface.

After a short introduction, we present the basics of device orientation notifications. To demonstrate the functionality of the XQDeviceOrientation class, we implement a simple application that displays a QWidget. The rotationChanged() signal emitted by the device orientation object will be connected to the update signal to the widget in order to draw an arrow on its surface. The arrow – due to the orientation information – will always point downwards on the *Y* axis of the device's coordinate system (i.e. the downward direction of the screen, as you can see in Figure 5.2). The implementation of this demonstration app is as follows:

```
1   #include "OrientationDemo.h"
2   #include "xqdeviceorientation.h"
3
4
5   OrientationDemo::OrientationDemo(QWidget *parent)
6       : QWidget(parent)
7   {
8           ui.setupUi(this);
9
10          // Create the orientation sensor object
11          XQDeviceOrientation* orientation = new XQDeviceOrientation(this);
12          orientation->open();
13          //specify the angle of the change to notify after
14          orientation->setResolution(5);
15
16          connect(orientation, SIGNAL(rotationChanged(int, int, int)),
17              this, SLOT(updateRotation(int, int, int)));
18
19          // Read the current orientation
20          rotation = orientation->xRotation();
21  }
22
23  void OrientationDemo::updateRotation(int rotx, int roty, int rotz) {
24
25          rotation=roty;
26          update();
27  }
28
29  void OrientationDemo::paintEvent(QPaintEvent* event)
30  {
31          //converting rotation into qreal value
32          qreal rotReal= 3.14 * rotation / 180;
33
34          QPainter painter(this);
35          QColor color(255, 255, 0);
36          painter.setBrush(color);
37          painter.setPen(color);
38          painter.translate(this->width()/2,this->height()/2);
39          painter.rotate(- rotReal);
40          painter.drawLine(0,-30,0,30);
41          painter.drawLine(-5,-30,5,-30);
42  }
43
44  OrientationDemo::~OrientationDemo() {}
```

After this short example, we now look at a demonstration of the second sensor class called XQAccelerationSensor, which offers an interface to access the device's acceleration sensor data. The sensor provides the calculated gravity values measured on the axis of the phone's own coordinate system (Figure 5.2). As you may recall, this sensor data can be accessed by registering filters rather than by the Qt signals and slots mechanism. The registered filters are stored in a stack and their `filter()` methods are called one after the other when a sensor event has been triggered. The filter method takes all the measured gravity values as integer parameters, which can be used by implementing the filter. It also has a return value, which indicates whether the received sensor data needs to be filtered out or not. This pattern can be used, for example, to filter rapidly triggered sensor events and pass the received gravity values to the application at a lower rate. Filters can let their parent application know about the filtered data by emitting signals or calling methods directly.

Note that the device orientation class introduced previously is actually a filter on the acceleration sensor, which calculates the actual rotation from the measured gravity values. Naturally, programmers can develop an acceleration filter of their own, in order to implement the special program functionality based on the accessed acceleration data. This can be accomplished by implementing the filter class based on the `XQAbstractAccelerationSensorFilter` interface and registering it using the sensor's `addFilter()` method. A filter can be any `QObject` sub-class, e.g. a simple form widget, just as the following code snippet demonstrates:

```
#include "AccelerationDemo.h"

AccelerationDemo::AccelerationDemo(QWidget *parent)
    : QWidget(parent)
{
    ui.setupUi(this);

    XQAccelerationSensor* accSensor= new XQAccelerationSensor(this);
    XQAccelerationDataPostFilter* postFilter =
    new XQAccelerationDataPostFilter();

    //init filter stack and start monitoring
    accSensor->open();
    accSensor->addFilter(*this);
    accSensor->addFilter(*postFilter);

    accSensor->startReceiving();
}

bool AccelerationDemo::filter(int& xAcceleration, int& yAcceleration, int
    & zAcceleration)
{
    //acceleration information received
    //you could use the received values for your own purposes
    //in this demo, we just simply show the values on a QLabel
    ui.lblAccelerationData->setText(
            "accX: "+QString::number(xAcceleration)+"\n"+
            "accY: "+QString::number(yAcceleration)+"\n"+
            "accZ: "+QString::number(zAcceleration));
```

```
31          //passing data through the filter
32      return false;
33  }
34
35  AccelerationDemo::~AccelerationDemo() {}
```

Note that, in addition to the widget, a second filter is added to the sensor. This filter is actually an XQAccelerationDataPostFilter instance, which is responsible for converting the raw acceleration values – which could be represented on a different scale by varying the version of the Symbian platform – to a standard range of -100 to $+100$, and modifying the sensor data so that the orientation of each acceleration axis is the same for all devices. Therefore, you should add a post-filter to the stack before your own filter instance in order to facilitate dealing with different types of devices.

7.2.9   Messaging API

Using the Qt programming framework in a mobile environment like Symbian requires access to those functionalities concerning wireless communication that any conventional mobile phone provides, such as telephony, contact data manipulation, messaging services, and so on. Many of these functions are already available in Qt from the previously introduced Mobile Extensions Library pack. The main advantage of this extension set is that developers can easily access the mobile device's services by writing Qt-style code, without knowing anything about any native Symbian API. To illustrate how a minimal effort is necessary to take advantage of these mobile services, we will demonstrate the functionality of one of these interfaces, the Messaging API.

The two main use cases regarding messaging are the following:

- Sending messages from your application.

- Registering a receiver slot in order to receive notification about incoming messages.

Currently three types of messages are supported by the API: short text messages (SMS), multimedia messages (MMS) and emails. All of these are handled consistently by the wrapper class called XQMessage, which provides an interface for querying and/or manipulating the attributes of a message, such as the receiver(s), message body, attachments, message type, etc. Therefore, this class allows you to construct your own custom message and send it using the XQMessaging class. Further, this class can also be used for connecting message receiver slots to its signals in order to process the contents of incoming messages. The received data is accessible through an instance of the XQMessage class.

After this brief summary, we will create a demo application that will provide a UI for sending short text messages. Its main form (as you can see in Table 7.7) will consist of text editors for providing the message body and the receiver's phone number, a button for sending a message and a QLabel item for displaying notifications about the status of the sending process.

We can realize the text message sending functionality by using the previously introduced classes. In the implementation of the click event handler we simply create a message object based on the provided properties, and send it using an instance of the XQMessaging class. The class implementation of the SMS text sending application is as follows:

Table 7.7   UI design of messaging example application.

QPlainTextEdit *editBody*	Message body
QLineEdit *editReceiver*	Message receiver
QPushButton *btnSend*	Sending the text
QLabel *lblStatus*	Status reporting

outcome

```
1
2  #include "MessagingExample.h"
3
4  MessagingExample::MessagingExample(QWidget *parent)
5      : QMainWindow(parent)
6  {
7
8          ui.setupUi(this);
9          ui.lblStatus->setText("Status: (not sent yet)");
10
11         //init XQMessaging
12         messaging = new XQMessaging(this);
13
14         connect(messaging, SIGNAL(error(XQMessaging::Error)),
15                     this, SLOT(sendingError(XQMessaging::Error)));
16
17
18  }
19
20  void MessagingExample::on_btnSend_clicked()
21  {
22         //send button click event handler
23
24         //creating the message
25         QString body=ui.editBody->toPlainText();
26         QStringList receivers;
27         receivers.append(ui.editReceiver->text());
28         XQMessage message(receivers, body);
29
30         //and sending the new XQMessage instance
```

```
31          messaging->send(message);
32
33          ui.lblStatus->setText("Status: (sent)");
34   }
35
36   void MessagingExample::sendingError(XQMessaging::Error err)
37   {
38          //called in case an error has been raised during sending
39
40          ui.lblStatus->setText(
41          "Status: (error "+QString::number(err)+")");
42   }
43
44   MessagingExample::~MessagingExample() {}
```

To conclude this section on messaging services, consider the following code snippet, which will demonstrate the method of registering a listener for incoming text messages. As described above, reception of the message is provided by the XQMessaging class. After setting up an instance, you have to connect the messageReceived(const XQMessage*) signal to your own slot implementation, in which you can process the received text message:

```
1
2    MessagingExample::MessagingExample(QWidget *parent)
3        : QMainWindow(parent)
4    {
5
6           messaging = new XQMessaging(this);
7
8           // connect slot for incoming message notification
9           connect(messaging, SIGNAL(messageReceived(const XQMessage&)),
10                          this, SLOT(messageReceived(const XQMessage&)));
11
12          connect(messaging, SIGNAL(error(XQMessaging::Error)),
13             this, SLOT(receivingError(XQMessaging::Error)));
14
15          // start receiving notifications
16          // the supplied parameters are for filtering the incoming
17                 messages
18          // and receive only SMS notifications
18          messaging->startReceiving(XQMessaging::MsgTypeSMS);
19
20   }
21
22   void MessagingExample::messageReceived(const XQMessage& message) {
23
24          //processing the incoming message
25          QString body=message.body();
26
```

```
27          // ...
28  }
29
30  void MessagingExample::receivingError(XQMessaging::Error err)
31  {
32          //called in case an error has been raised during receiving
33          ui.lblStatus->setText(
34          "Status: (error "+QString::number(err)+")");
35  }
```

Note that the XQMessaging class – in addition to startReceiving() – also has a method called stopReceiving(), which must be called if no further notifications are needed. The example above does not use this method; therefore, notifications will be received until termination of the application.

7.2.10   Camera API

Nowadays many mobile devices come with a built-in camera, and mobile application developers might want to use it in their Qt programs. Naturally, such functionality cannot be implemented in any of the standard cross-platform Qt modules. To access the device functionality of the camera, developers can use the extension classes which are available in the Camera API. The classes are called XQViewFinderWidget and XQCamera. The first one is for displaying a camera preview image on the UI, while the second one provides a programming interface for taking photos and getting the resulting JPEG image.

The procedure for obtaining the camera image is as follows. First, you have to initialize the camera device and connect its slots and signals to your application. Picture taking is accessible through the corresponding capture() slot of the camera class; the processed image can be reached by connecting a slot to the captureCompleted(QByteArray) or captureCompleted(QImage*) signal of the class. In order to show the camera preview image on the UI, you also need to initialize the viewfinder widget and connect the camera's cameraReady() signal to the start() slot of the viewfinder. Following these steps provides a basic camera application with capabilities for displaying the preview image and receiving the data of the captured photo. After obtaining the resulting image as a byte array or a QImage object, you may use it for your own purposes.

The following Qt program, called CameraDemo, demonstrates how you can create a simple photo taker application. Its UI (as you can see in Table 7.8) consists of the camera preview widget mentioned above and a button which could be used for taking a picture based on the current preview frame. The free space on the widget's surface will be used for drawing the captured image. In order to do this, we will simply store the image in the implementation of the slot that handles the captured picture and request a widget repaint. The reimplementation of the form's paintEvent() method will be responsible for drawing the last stored image – if there is any – on the surface of the form:

CameraDemo.h:

```
1  #ifndef CAMERADEMO_H
2  #define CAMERADEMO_H
3
```

Table 7.8 UI design of camera example.

XQViewFinderWidget *viewFinder*	Displays camera preview picture
QPushButton *btnCapture*	Triggers picture taking
Place for drawing captured image	

outcome

```
4   #include <QtGui/QMainWindow>
5   #include <QPaintEvent>
6   #include <QPainter>
7   #include <QColor>
8   #include <QImage>
9   #include "ui_CameraDemo.h"
10  #include "xqcamera.h"
11
12  class CameraDemo : public QMainWindow
13  {
14      Q_OBJECT
15
16  public:
17          CameraDemo(QWidget *parent = 0);
18          ~CameraDemo();
19
20  private:
21          //variables for image drawing
22          int IMAGE_VIEW_WIDTH;
23          int IMAGE_VIEW_HEIGHT;
24          QPoint drawTo;
25
26          //hold the captured image
27          QImage* capturedImage;
28
29          //camera device
30          XQCamera* camera;
31
32      Ui::CameraDemoClass ui;
```

```
33
34   protected:
35          void paintEvent(QPaintEvent * event);
36
37   private slots:
38          void imageCaptured(QImage * image);
39
40   };
41
42   #endif // CAMERADEMO_H
```

CameraDemo.cpp:

```
1    #include "CameraDemo.h"
2
3    CameraDemo::CameraDemo(QWidget *parent)
4        : QMainWindow(parent)
5    {
6          ui.setupUi(this);
7
8          //initialize variables for image drawing
9          IMAGE_VIEW_WIDTH = this->width() - 10;
10         IMAGE_VIEW_HEIGHT = IMAGE_VIEW_WIDTH * 3 / 4;
11         drawTo.setX(5);
12         drawTo.setY(this->height() - 5 - IMAGE_VIEW_HEIGHT);
13
14         //initialize camera device
15         camera=new XQCamera(this);
16         camera->setCaptureSize(QSize(640,480));
17
18         //connect the button's clicked signal to the capture slot
19         connect(ui.btnCapture, SIGNAL(clicked()),
20         camera, SLOT(capture()));
21
22         //connect the camera's captureCompleted signal
23         connect(camera, SIGNAL(captureCompleted(QImage*)),
24         this, SLOT(imageCaptured(QImage*)));
25
26         //initialize the view finder widget
27         ui.viewFinder->setCamera(*camera);
28         ui.viewFinder->setViewfinderSize(QSize(128,96));
29
30         //starting preview when camera is ready
31         connect(camera, SIGNAL(cameraReady()),
32         ui.viewFinder, SLOT(start()));
33
34   }
35
36   void CameraDemo::paintEvent(QPaintEvent* event)
```

```
37  {
38          //main window repaint
39          //if we have a captured image,
40          //we draw it on the surface of the form
41          if(capturedImage) {
42
43                  QPainter painter(this);
44                  painter.translate(drawTo);
45                  painter.scale(
46          1.0 * IMAGE_VIEW_WIDTH / capturedImage->width() ,
47          1.0 * IMAGE_VIEW_HEIGHT / capturedImage->height());
48                  painter.drawImage(QPoint(0,0),*capturedImage);
49
50          }
51
52  }
53
54
55  void CameraDemo::imageCaptured(QImage * image)
56  {
57          //called by camera device, when capture is completed
58
59          capturedImage=image; //storing the captured image
60          update(); //requesting repaint in order to draw the image
61  }
62
63  CameraDemo::~CameraDemo() {}
```

7.2.11 Location API

Since mobile services based on location information are becoming more widely used, accessing position data on mobile devices has become a more important issue. With the Location API extension of the Qt Application Framework, developers are able to access the location information provided by various sets of technologies like the built-in or attached GPS receiver, or the network-based location provider. The wrapper class called XQLocation hides the details of the technology actually used and provides the data in a standard format: the location information is represented as coordinate values of the current latitude, longitude and altitude.

The standard way to access location information in Qt for Symbian is to instantiate the XQLocation class, call its open() method to initialize the underlying provider, and finally to listen for location change notifications in a corresponding slot connected to the location class locationChanged() signal. If you are interested only in certain location values (e.g. elevation or speed), alternatively you can connect to the slots specialized for emitting the required information, such as speedChanged(), altitudeChanged(), etc. It might also be useful to connect a slot to the signal of the location provider onStatusChanged(XQLocation::DeviceStatus) in order to be informed about the current availability of the provider and change the behaviour of the application if necessary.

The following code snippet demonstrates the procedure for requesting location information in practice. The demo application is a simple form, the UI of which consists of a single QLabel called lblLocation, which will be used for displaying the coordinate values obtained. As you can see, we initialize the XQLocation class in the constructor of our form and connect our slot called updateLocation() to the location changed signal. Finally, in the implementation of the slot we simply refresh the displayed text of the label based on the received parameters after converting the double values to a displayable form with four-digit precision:

```cpp
#include "LocationDemo.h"
#include "xqlocation.h"

LocationDemo::LocationDemo(QWidget *parent)
    : QMainWindow(parent)
{
        ui.setupUi(this);

        //initialize provider
        XQLocation* location=new XQLocation(this);

        //connecting the location changed slot
        connect(location,
        SIGNAL(locationChanged(double, double, double, float)), this,
            SLOT(updateLocation(double, double, double, float)));


//opening the provider
        if (location->open() != XQLocation::NoError) {
        ui.lblLocation->setText("Error opening location provider.");
        return;
        }

        //requesting updates when location changes
        //note that calling startUpdates(int) instead causes
        //requesting location information periodically
        location->startUpdates();

}

void LocationDemo::updateLocation( double latitude, double longitude,
        double altitude, float speed)
{

        ui.lblLocation->setText(
                "Latitude: "+QString::number(latitude, 'f', 4)+"\n"+
                "Longitude: "+QString::number(longitude, 'f', 4)+"\n"+
                "Altitude: "+QString::number(altitude, 'f', 4)+"\n"+
                "Speed: "+QString::number(speed, 'f', 4));
```

```
41  }
42
43  LocationDemo::~LocationDemo() {}
```

Note that it is also possible to request updated location data only once (as a single request). In this case, you should use a singe call of the `requestUpdate()` method instead of `startUpdates()`.

INDEX